BEHOLD THE MYSTERY

A DEEPER UNDERSTANDING OF THE CATHOLIC MASS

MARK HART

the WORD among us® Press

Published by The Word Among Us Press
7115 Guilford Drive, Suite 100
Frederick, Maryland 21704
www.wau.org

18 17 16 15 14   1 2 3 4 5

ISBN: 978-1-59325-228-1
eISBN: 978-1-59325-463-6

Scripture texts used in this work are taken from The Catholic
Edition of Revised Standard Version Bible, copyright © 1965,
1966 by the Division of Christian Education of the National
Council of the Churches of Christ in the United States of America.
Used with permission. All rights reserved.

Cover design by John Hamilton Designs

Artwork credit: Pierre Hubert Subleyras, (1699-1749)
Saint Basil celebrating the Mass in Greek Rite before the Emperor.
Location: S. Maria degli Angeli, Rome, Italy
Photo Credit: Scala/Art Resource, NY

Made and printed in the United States of America

Library of Congress Control Number: 2014931520

BEHOLD THE MYSTERY

A DEEPER UNDERSTANDING OF THE CATHOLIC MASS

To all of the Catholic priests of God, who so humbly and courageously bring Christ to his people each day:

Thank you all for your dedication, your sacrifice, and your unwavering fidelity to the Lord and his Church. Your response to God's call not only inspires us, it saves us.

May Our Lady hold you firmly in her arms and the priesthood safely in her mantle. And may the Spirit of God continue to challenge and empower you to become who you were designed by the Father to be. Never forget the privilege it is to serve in the vineyard of the Lord, and may you do so with great joy.

Contents

Introduction

If we really understood the Mass,
we would die of joy.
—St. John Vianney

The lottery jackpot had climbed to an astounding $365 million. All over the country, people tried to increase their odds of winning at least a piece of the pie by banding together and buying tickets in large quantities. But on that night when the numbered balls began to fall, each number revealing a dwindling group of potential winners, hearts all over the country sank as well. In the end, on a cold day in February 2006, eight employees of a Nebraska meat-packing plant walked away with the prize money.

What would you do if you were the one holding the winning lottery ticket? Would you retire? Would you buy a new home? How much would you give away to the less fortunate, and what charities would benefit from your good fortune?

Now what if you had the winning ticket, but you had to walk to the lottery office to claim your winnings. How far would you be willing to walk? One hundred miles? Two hundred? How about one thousand? What if it were the dead of winter? The dog days of summer? How far would you be willing to go and what would you be willing to endure to collect a prize that is worth so much?

While the analogy is far-fetched, it reveals a deep truth—our willingness to be uncomfortable for something is directly proportional to the value we place upon its worth.

People will brave biting cold or intense rain for hours on end to cheer their favorite team on to victory. People will camp out in tents on concrete for days to be the first in line for movie or concert tickets. These examples, and countless others, reaffirm a profound truth offered to us by Christ himself, namely, "For where your treasure is, there will your heart be also" (Matthew 6:21).

God has given us a gift far more valuable than those lottery winnings, far more than we can ever comprehend. God has given us the gift of himself at Mass. How much value do we place on it? How much are we willing to give him in return?

Passion for the Liturgy

I've had many conversations over the years with those who are confused, bored, disinterested, or disengaged with the Mass or who left the Church many years ago. Within these pages, I want to enlighten your mind, but above all, I want to stir up your soul. I believe that if we could all engage the liturgy with the passion of our souls, we would quickly awaken to the great gift, the priceless treasure, the pearl of great price that has always been before us but that has sometimes been mistaken for costume jewelry. With the Holy Spirit's help, I hope to achieve two things in this book, as seen from the title.

First, I'm writing it with the hope of helping all of us—young and old, lifelong Catholics, and those new to the family—to "behold" this mystery of the Mass. The idea here is to simplify what can seem so complicated; not to solve the mystery, but to reframe it in such a way that we can really engage in it. We will be looking at the liturgy from many different angles.

Some approach the liturgy strictly as sacrifice, others as celebration, still others merely as "what Catholics are supposed to do." All are correct, yet all these perspectives are supposed to weave together into one fabric and offer context. Pull just one thread, and sooner or later the vision of the whole will unravel. The Mass is deep mystery and high drama, but in the end it is a simple sacrifice—God for us—and a simple meal between God and us.

> I pray that this book can make the Mass come to life for us in a new and personal way.

Second, I pray that this book can make the Mass come to life for us in a new and personal way. We are physical beings and visual people. Through the Mass and the sacraments, God interacts with us and engages us in physical and visual ways. We are also a people who love to hear and share through simple stories. Throughout the Gospels, and indeed the entire Bible, God reveals himself and his love to us through the power of the story. My hope is that each chapter will offer you physical examples—memorable stories and practical ideas—that you can call upon in the months and years to come. As you seek to enter more deeply into the mystery of the Mass, you will come to see your own "story" wrapped up within God's story and within the story and mission of the Church. I believe that you can find your story within God's story. Whether you are at a scarcely populated weekday morning liturgy, an overflowing Christmas Eve Mass, or a Sunday Mass during Ordinary Time, you can recall the meaning of the Church's journey within your own.

What Is the Mass?

Of course, there is a danger in writing a book about the Mass, namely, that you can't make everyone happy. There have been many books on the topic—many that delve into theological concepts in a far deeper and exhaustive way. This is not one of those books. I am in no way attempting to say everything about the Catholic Mass; I am attempting to say *some things* about it. I'm not a liturgist, nor am I a priest. I am a husband, a father, a lay minister, and, most important, a son of God. I'm writing from the perspective of one in the pews, not one in the sanctuary.

Some will judge the merit of this book by whether it supports the Mass in Latin or in the *Novus Ordo* (ordinary language). Some will search through these pages to see whether I advocate an organ and cantor or a music ministry with guitars and drums. I'll address neither within the book. We need to get back to what the Mass *is* and not get sidetracked with how it is carried out. Truthfully, some in our Church won't be happy until Latin is the only Mass celebrated, while others won't be happy until every Mass has a laser light show. We don't need pews filled with people more Catholic than the pope any more than we need pews filled with those unaware of what the Church teaches liturgically or what it offers us all intellectually. Instead, we need people whose hearts and minds engage with the liturgy, whose souls are nourished by the Eucharistic Lord, and who are ready for mission when they exit the doors of the church.

The Mass offers us all a unique opportunity to see things as God sees them. We are invited into the throne room of heaven for an hour each Sunday to worship alongside the angels. We are being ushered into the upper room of Holy Thursday to recline at the Lord's table. We are on the mount of Calvary as our Lord offers himself to the Father on our behalf. Make no mistake: the Mass is not about God "reaching down" to earth as much as it is about us being swept up into heaven. Our Sunday worship is not merely about devotion; it's about reception.

So how do we go from Mass being less a ritualistic exercise and more a relationship-based encounter? What is necessary for this change in perspective and in practice?

Like anything in the Catholic faith, it all begins with a prayer. So say a prayer now, before turning the page. Ask the same Holy Spirit who inspired the Sacred Scriptures and inspires and guides our Catholic Church to open your eyes and heart so that you might treasure the mystery enough to behold it in a new way.

CHAPTER ONE

The Elephant in the Sanctuary: Understanding the Problem

If only we knew how God regards this Sacrifice,
we would risk our lives to be present at a single Mass.
—*St. Padre Pio*

The room, filled beyond capacity, was quite warm. The light flickering from the candles could scarcely keep tired eyes from beginning to close. The homily, though undoubtedly poignant and passionate, showed no signs of stopping as the clock approached the midnight hour.

Toward the back of the room, a young man who had been slowly nodding off finally succumbed to the rhythmic speech patterns of the preacher. What began as a light nap during a long homily quickly escalated, because Eutychus not only fell into a deep sleep but fell down (three stories) to a painful death. Apparently, the last seat in the house—on a windowsill—was not the best choice after all.

You may have felt like you were going to die during a long homily. Eutychus actually did.

How embarrassing too, because the great missionary, St. Paul, was the one preaching when this tragedy occurred. Fortunately, he saved face in the city of Troas (and undoubtedly bolstered his reputation) when he later restored Eutychus to life—and all were relieved. If you've never read this story (Acts

20:7-12), I highly recommend you do; it's both captivating and humorous.

Whether Eutychus was bored or just tired, it's hard to say. But the fact that we can identify with this story says something. So let's call out the elephant in the room, or in the sanctuary, as it were: many Catholics find the Mass boring and/or confusing. That is not to say that they doubt its importance; just that, when all is said and done, the Mass is often not described as dynamic or engaging or life changing by most within the pews.

What Is Your Experience of the Mass?

Eutychus notwithstanding, what was Mass like for those in the early Church? It was undoubtedly an exciting time to be a Christian, and by exciting, I mean dangerous. Reports of Christ's crucifixion had spread throughout Judea and Galilee, but news of his supposed resurrection must have spread even faster. Thousands of Jews (and soon tens of thousands) stopped worshipping on the Sabbath (Saturday), as had been their custom for thousands of years, and seemingly overnight began to gather on "the first day of the week" (Sunday) to commemorate the miraculous rising of this itinerant Nazarene carpenter (Acts 20:7).

Under threat of persecution and the promise of a similar martyrdom, the followers of Jesus began to gather in secret behind locked doors in homes and, eventually, even in catacombs, to participate in the Eucharistic sacrifice instituted by Christ in the upper room on the eve of Good Friday. For Christ's early followers, Mass was a matter of life and death, literally. Participating in Mass could be life threatening, not just life offering. Yet it was at the altar table that the young Church understood its new identity in Christ and was empowered to go forth and share that new identity with a world in need.

Is this *your experience* of the Mass every Sunday? Does it evoke this level of "life-or-death" joy and expectation from you and from your children? It certainly didn't for me or for my family when I was growing up.

So what has changed since the dawn of the Church? What is the modern Church lacking? These questions deserves serious reflection and discussion. For if the Mass and, specifically, the Eucharist is "the source and summit" of our Catholic faith, as the Second Vatican Council has written (*Lumen Gentium*, 11), shouldn't it show in our schedules, parish budgets, and, most notably, in the look on our faces?

The truth of Christ has not changed. Jesus Christ is the same "yesterday and today and fo rever" (Hebrews 13:8), and neither has the basic form of the Mass. For two thousand years, Christians have gathered together to celebrate the Eucharist. We hear of it in the Acts of the Apostles: "They devoted themselves to the apostles' teaching and fellowship, to the breaking of bread and the prayers" (2:42).

Think about all the great saints over the last two thousand years. Despite being separated by centuries, continents, languages, political and socioeconomic challenges, and cultural differences, what did they all have in common? They encountered grace through the hands of Christ's same priesthood, just as we do. They received absolution, consumed his Body and Blood, and came together as a Church, just as we do. The locations varied, some legal, many not. The languages varied, some ancient and some modern. The world powers varied, but all these saints came under the kingship of Christ. Consistently, for two thousand years, on battlefields and in basilicas, in castles and in convents, in homes and in hospitals, in parishes and in prisons, the same words of consecration, the same sacrifice has been offered. The same Church, with billions of different faces, has uttered the same profession of faith: "Amen."

The Mass is not lacking; we are.

We in the modern Church hear the same Scripture readings proclaimed and the same words of consecration, yet countless souls exit their local parish churches unshaken and unstirred. While it's difficult to substantiate, it's been said that the largest denomination of Christians in America is fallen-away Catholics. The view from the pew—and even within entire dioceses—can appear bleak in many circumstances. While U.S. dioceses endure the pains of parish closings and consolidations, there are entire cathedrals in Europe being dismantled, auctioned off, and sold for alternative purposes. A church I once visited is now being used as a parking garage for bicycles. Holy ground, where the chains of sin fell and where angels tread, is now lined with bike locks, chains, and tire tread.

The bad news is that many souls have departed. The good news is that each year many souls are converted. Perhaps the best news is that God is merciful. All the baptized who have left are constantly urged to come home, confess their sins, reconcile with their Father, and rejoin their sisters and brothers around the (altar) dinner table once again. It's one of the constant themes of Pope Francis.

The Mass is not lacking; we are. That is not to say that the liturgy in most places could not improve; it most certainly could. It is to say, however, that God is not the problem. But our perspective can be.

Entertainment Versus Mystery

My daughter once asked me, "Daddy, why is Mass sooo boorrring?!?"

You've heard it asked before too. In fact, you've probably asked it yourself at some point in your life. As sad a question as it is to hear from your own child, one has to admit that it's valid. If you don't know what's going on at Mass, it really can feel like a Catholic version of low-impact aerobics: stand, sit, stand, sit, stand, sit, kneel, and then exit as quickly as possible to get the best selection of donuts.

Have you ever been bored during the Catholic Mass? Have you ever strained to stay awake as a homily dragged on? Have you ever been left with the impression that those worshipping around you were less than enthused to be at Mass at all? I have. On some Sundays, I still do. Still, I have to remember that there is more to the Mass than meets the eye. So when my daughter inquired why Mass was "so boring," I answered her question with another question. "Tell me what the Mass is. Answer that, and then I'll tell you why 'it's boring.'"

There's nothing wrong with wanting entertainment in life. In fact, God designed us with five senses, and so we are hardwired with a desire to have those senses engaged. That engagement is often found most directly through what we consider "entertainment." What about our souls, though? At what point do our souls, and not just our bodies, become engaged in worship? How do our intellect, our sensory perception, and, most important, our souls all unite in a way that transcends earth and encounters heaven?

Entertainment is often the replacement when mystery is lacking. When people ask why the Catholic Mass is not more entertaining, the shortest answer is because it is high mystery—not a mystery to be "solved" but rather a mystery to behold. We are a Church steeped in mystery because we are a faith that is born out of mystery—the Holy Trinity, to be exact.

Are we just modern-day versions of Eutychus, well-intentioned but overtired? After all, the "spirit indeed is willing, but the flesh is weak" (Mark 14:38). Or could it be something deeper? Could it be that what we've lost is our appreciation of mystery? Could it be that our highly technological and screen-based age has slowly desensitized and overstimulated us to such an extent that we've lost our sense of wonder or ability to contemplate? Is God to be found in the noise, the bright lights and flickering images, or in the stillness?

As difficult as it is for me to embrace the silence most days, the prophet Elijah and the psalmist would attest to the fact that while God *can* speak through the noise and the screens, his medium of choice tends to be the silence (1 Kings 19:11-13; Psalm 46:10). Of course, God uses any and all means (and mediums) to get our attention. After all, Christ was adept at using everything in his proximity to catechize, be it a vine, a fig tree, lilies, or birds. But note how many times the Gospels record our Lord withdrawing to the mountain or garden for silent prayer time.

Why doesn't God just make Mass more entertaining? After all, we worship a God who breathes creativity. Consider the sunrise and coffee beans, giraffes and platypuses, thunder and lightning, avocados and chili peppers. Our Creator is a force of creativity; our God has style. Why not more flash and dazzle in the sanctuary? Why not more visual stimulation? Why

> We need to open the eyes of our souls
> and not just our heads.

not more crowd participation? Why not movie-theater seating in the churches? Why doesn't the Holy Spirit just work a little harder through the leaders of the Church to ensure that the faithful are more engaged?

These questions are all just natural derivations of the same question posed by my daughter, and the answer to these questions is found in my answer to her: Tell me what the Mass *is*, and I'll tell you why "it's boring."

Seeing the Mass from God's Perspective

We need to open the eyes of our souls and not just our heads. If the people of Nazareth taught us anything, it's that Christ could be right in front of you and you still might not recognize him. They weren't expecting much from the local carpenter's kid. And why do you think that Jesus, like John the Baptist before him, was so disliked by the Pharisees? There were several reasons, but at its root it was because Jesus didn't meet their criteria. He didn't measure up to their preconceived notions and standards for a messiah. When we tell God how we are supposed to worship, when creation tells the Creator how things ought to be, all hell breaks loose. (See Genesis 3 if you don't believe me.)

Throughout salvation history, time and time again, God not only meets our needs, he exceeds them. Remember the hungry masses and the boy with only a few loaves and fish? How about the woman with the hemorrhage or the man born blind? What about the entire human race, dead in sin before Christ's victorious and heroic death on the cross? God exceeds our needs—every day.

Whenever we try to fit him into our mold, however, that's when the ark of salvation begins to take on water. God meets our needs, yes, but not on our terms. Thinking that is how it should be is high folly. God shouldn't form-fit himself to our desires, and we shouldn't want him to do so. He is the God of the universe, not the genie in our bottle. Christ's power is more magnificent in his self-emptying on the cross and in the Eucharistic bread than it ever could be in laser light shows or multiple video screens. The Spirit might appear as a dove, but that doesn't mean he's fit for a cage. Entertainment might be what many want, but God is more concerned with what we *need*.

To understand God's plan for our salvation and his desire for weekly intimacy in the liturgy, we must look to his design and his revelation as entrusted to us in Sacred Scripture, for the Mass, from beginning to end, is inherently and inseparably biblical. Like an iceberg whose mass is 90 percent submerged, the Catholic Mass has a depth and volume and density that requires us to look beneath the surface that we see on Sunday. To really gain the proper perspective of the liturgy, we have to understand not just "our" own perspective but God's hope for it from the beginning.

Before we can discuss how important the Mass is, however, we actually need to take a step back and view the importance (or lack thereof) of the Sabbath in general.

Questions for Reflection and Discussion

1. What is one word you would use to describe your normal experience of the Mass?

2. What might be inhibiting you from entering more deeply into the Mass? Why?

3. Do you feel that most people attending Sunday Mass understand the totality of what is going on within the liturgy? Why or why not? Give an example to explain your answer.

4. What is something you, your parish, or your pastor could do to help the Mass-goer engage more fully in the liturgy? Offer examples and discuss.

CHAPTER TWO

Rest Assured:
Understanding the Sabbath

*All the good works in the world are not equal to the Holy
Sacrifice of the Mass because they are the works of men; but
the Mass is the work of God.*
—St. John Vianney

once heard a child ask his vacation Bible school teacher, "Why
did God have to rest on the seventh day?" It was an insightful
question for such a young child. The teacher's answer, though
well-intentioned, left much to be desired. She replied, "Well, . . .
because he was so tired after creating so much in such a short
amount of time."

The teacher may not have felt that the boy could comprehend more, but that young child was now viewing our God as
having limitations. Over time, such a view could prove treacherous. Sadly, the teacher's view of God is not rare. We often
apply limitations to God because we think of him being more
like us than us like him. Did Christ fall asleep during the storm
at sea? Yes, he did, in the stern on a cushion, to be exact (Mark
4:38). That incident notwithstanding, God the Father does
not require "sleep." To clarify, God didn't rest on the Sabbath
because *he* needed it. He commands sabbath rest because *we*
need it.

Creation: God's Act of Love

God is pure love. The Trinity, as such, is the perfect expression of love. The Lover (God the Father) so deeply loves the Beloved (Christ the Son) that their mutual love is personified in the Holy Spirit. As such, Love needs a recipient of that love. The act and art of creation, the very fact that we are alive, is a living expression of the love of God. Every creative step, every "day" of creation, reveals something more about God, his eternal love, and the intricacy of his perfect and divine design. (Of course, the Church does

> The act and art of creation, the very fact that we are alive, is a living expression of the love of God.

not teach that we must interpret Genesis chapters 1 through 11 "literally," that is to say, "unscientifically." Using allegory, the writers of Genesis were far more concerned with communicating the why of creation than the how.)

Note also that every stage of creation grows in complexity. As Genesis reveals the creative order, we see increasing detail as well:

Day One: Light/Darkness
Day Two: Water
Day Three: Dry Land/Water/Vegetation
Day Four: Sun/Moon/Stars
Day Five: Birds/Fish

Day Six: Animals/Man
Day Seven: Sabbath (Rest)

We begin with light and darkness on Day One and reach creation's pinnacle on Day Six with the creation of man. Notice that on the sixth day, God didn't stop with the creation of the animals, which would have been understandable. No, God got even more creative than the rhinoceros and the kangaroo. As complexity grew, so did our blessedness.

> So God created msn in his own image, in the image of God he created him; male and female he created them. And God blessed them, and God said to them, "Be fruitful and multiply, and fill the earth and subdue it; and have dominion over the fish of the sea and over the birds of the air and over every living thing that moves upon the earth.". . . And God saw everything that he had made, and behold, it was very good. And there was evening and there was morning, the sixth day.
>
> Thus the heavens and the earth were finished, and all the host of them. And on the seventh day God finished his work which he had done, and he rested on the seventh day from all his work which he had done. So God blessed the seventh day and hallowed it, because on it God rested from all his work which he had done in creation. (Genesis 1:27-28, 31; 2:1-3)

If Adam was created on the "sixth day" (Genesis 1:31) and was then cast into a deep sleep, logic follows that the seventh day now functioned not only as Adam's sabbath but also as his wedding day. When creation's first "anesthesia" wore off, man awoke with a gorgeous wife and a sore side—a small price to pay by anyone's standards. In his best-selling book, *A Father Who Keeps His Promises*, noted biblical scholar Dr. Scott Hahn framed the marriage in early Genesis in this way:

> There's no reason to suppose that Adam lived a long time as a bachelor. In terms of narrative time, his second day began when he woke up from his deep sleep, which also happened to be the Sabbath Day sanctified by God. So Adam's first full day may have been both a day of sabbath rest and betrothal, for Eve and himself, as marriage covenant partners. From a narrative perspective, the Sabbath may be seen as the sign of two closely related covenants: between God and creation, and Adam and Eve.[1]

So in essence, the Sabbath doesn't just celebrate God's desire for man to rest in him but also his desire to bless and breathe life within the marriage relationship of man and woman. After all, marriage wasn't man's idea; it was God's. God, the author of marriage, designed it to mirror the love of the Holy Trinity, with the lover (husband) and beloved (wife) bearing fruit in new life—children. This type of complete love and total self-gift is what marks marriage not as a piece of paper or legally binding agreement but as a covenant.

What's a Covenant?

A covenant is a sacred, familial bond between God and man or between people. It is far more than a contract. A covenant is more than doing mutually beneficial favors or exchanging goods and services. A covenant is a complete exchange of self. A covenant is a living embodiment of love, teaching us not only how to give but how to receive love. When God enters into a covenant with Adam and Eve, he is offering all of himself to them and inviting Adam and Eve to offer themselves back to him in return.

After our first parents broke their end of the covenant through sin, there was a debt to be paid. God held up his end of the covenant, but we broke ours. Shortly thereafter, with Cain's displeasing sacrifice to God and murder of his brother Abel (Genesis 4), things went from bad to worse. As time went on, God formed new covenants—with Noah, with Abraham, with Moses, and with David—all of which were eventually broken as well.

God entered into a covenant with Adam and Eve and marked that covenant with the Sabbath as a reminder to them. You may be wondering, however: why was the Sabbath used as the reminder? Why not a ring like we use today? Why not some other outward sacrifice? What does the covenant have to do with the seventh day, the day of rest?

Biblically speaking, numbers matter. For example, there were twelve sons of Jacob and twelve tribes of Israel, and Jesus chose twelve apostles among his disciples. Moses spent forty days atop Mount Sinai, the Israelites wandered forty years in the desert, and Jesus spent forty days fasting through temptations in the wilderness.

Why is the seventh day so significant? The number seven is equated with completion. And for the ancient Israelites, a group of people who were intimately aware of the depth and sacredness of covenant oaths, the number seven described far more than "a handshake deal" or a written contract. The

Hebrew word for swearing an oath is *sheba*, and it is based on the word for "seven." Taken literally, to enter into a sworn oath could be known as "sevening" yourself. (See Genesis 21:27-32 for another example of this.)

In this understanding, the Sabbath (seventh day) places us within the covenant in a natural rhythm of not only rest but of praise, worship, and intimacy. In this way, we can "renew" our covenant and our promise to God each and every week, without fail. Keeping the Sabbath holy can be likened to a couple (Adam and Eve, in this case) renewing their wedding vows to one another and to God, entering far more deeply and intimately into his covenant by inviting him into their own (marriage) covenant.

Celebrating the Sabbath: Weekly or Weakly?

So how do you live out the covenant that God has made with us through Jesus Christ, the new covenant born out of his body and blood? How do you renew it each week? What sets your Sabbath apart, aside from rearranging the work/sports/family schedule so that you can swing by the church for an hour once a week? What does this covenant between God and us "look like" in a practical sense?

First, our covenant with God, while it begins with our Sunday Sabbath, must go beyond that one hour each week at church. Do you pray outside of Mass and beyond grace before meals? Do you pray as a family? Does your weekend revolve around Mass or around sports and activities? How do you keep God in first place every day and each week?

A husband and wife do not renew their vows only on their anniversary; they renew them each and every day in the ways they seek the other before themselves. Every morning and every evening, an earthly father demonstrates to his children what is most important by the way he spends his time, not only on Sundays, but every day of the week.

Does God get our best or what's left of our time?

Second, not only should we make it to Mass each Sunday, but we must actually "rest." Do your weekly duties and chores, such as bills and cleaning and yard work, all find their way to your Sunday task list? Certainly, these things need to be done, but is there a way to fit them in on other days of the week? If the answer is no, it may be time to rethink how many activities and commitments you (and your family) may be involved in. A Sabbath without rest is no Sabbath at all (Mark 2:27-28).

Does God get our best or what's left of our time? And for those who have to work on Sundays, what other day functions as your Sabbath now? Priests and those in active ministry must find an alternate day for their sabbath rest. Let us never forget that "keeping the Sabbath holy" is more than just going to church for an hour. We must rest, pray, laugh, and be present to family and friends. That is what transforms a Sunday to a Sabbath.

How much different would your week look if you spent not just an hour at Mass but the entire day entering more deeply into the presence of God with your family and friends? How much better would your Monday morning be if your Sunday was more than church in the morning and running errands in the afternoon? Not that there's anything wrong with getting your errands done, but are they done at the expense of sacred time with family and God?

So God commands us to honor the Sabbath, not just to save us from the (often disordered) world, but to save us from ourselves. Sunday doesn't just prepare us for the week ahead; it prepares us for eternity.

Finally, think about the quality of your covenant relationship with God. Do you approach him with your brokenness, fears, and sins, or merely with your needs, wants, and expectations? Intimacy welcomes both, but the former speaks to a desire for relationship while the latter points toward a desired resolution. God awaits us, daily, to go to him. He bids us, weekly (at least), to come and encounter him in the Mass. To enrich and renew our covenant relationship with him, we need to do both.

If you want to live as a Christian, get comfortable with being uncomfortable, and if you're afraid of what following God might require of you, you may want to skip the next chapter.

Questions for Reflection and Discussion

1. Beyond attending Mass, what are some examples of ways you "keep holy" the Sabbath?

2. What are some things you could do differently in your home, relationships, and/or schedule to enter more fully into the Sabbath?

3. Do you ever stop to consider that Sunday Mass isn't just about us spending time with God but about God's desire to spend time around the table with us? Why or why not? How does this perspective enhance or change your view of God as Father? Discuss.

4. Have you ever thought of your relationship with God in terms of a covenant? How does that change how you think about it? How you think about Sundays?

CHAPTER THREE

Sky High: Understanding Worship

The Mass is the most perfect form of prayer.
—Pope Paul VI

My heart beat at the rapid pace of a cheetah in full sprint. Sweat flowed from my brow like a faucet left running. My lungs burned as I gasped for breath in the thinning air. My legs, once energetic and strong, now felt like overcooked spaghetti dangling from my torso. My idea to scale the mountain had moved from inspired to idiotic. I was only fifteen hundred feet up, and the summit was nowhere in site. The higher I hiked, the lower I felt.

Between breaths, I began to wonder: why did God create mountains to begin with? And what had possessed me to want to "conquer" this stupid pile of rocks? I persisted, however, and when I (finally) ascended to the summit of the mountain, twenty-seven hundred feet in the air (that's a half-mile high, people), I prayed two prayers. First, I prayed for a helicopter ride home. Second, I prayed in thanksgiving to the Creator for the amazing view from the mountaintop. It was breathtaking, literally and emotionally. I prayed in gratitude as well for the beauty of all creation, which is designed to point us back to the Creator.

Since an air rescue was not in God's providential cards for me that day, I descended the mountain, legs weary but heart quite full. During my descent back down to earth, I was struck by how many amazing biblical events occur in Scripture on mountains. Think about it:

- Where does Noah's ark rest after the waters cease? A mountain.
- Where does Abraham prepare to sacrifice his only son, Isaac? A mountain.
- Where does Moses receive the Ten Commandments? A mountain.
- Where does David seek to build God's Temple? A mountain.
- Where does Elijah encounter God most profoundly? A mountain.
- Where does Christ give his most famous sermon? A mount(ain).
- Where does Jesus most often go to pray? A mountain.
- Where does our Lord offer his very body and blood on the cross? A mountain.
- Where does Jesus ascend by his own power? A mountain.

These are just to name a few. Mountains don't just play an important role in the artistic beauty we call landscape but in the backdrop of our story of salvation as well.

At this point, you might be wondering, "What does a mountain have to do with the Mass? My church is built on a rolling hill in the suburbs."

The Mountain and the Molehill

While it may not seem so on the surface, what happens at the obscure parish on a mundane molehill at an unnamed city is, in reality, a mountaintop experience with its summit in heaven, an invitation into the very throne room of God for a face-to-face, intimate encounter with Jesus Christ, our Lord and Savior. But the mountain looks like a molehill when those invited up the mountain are unaware of what is transpiring at the top. You must be willing to put in the effort to scale the summit. That's the only way you and others can gain a new perspective atop the mountain of Christ's Mass.

Unfortunately, our earthly eyes inhibit our heaven-bent hearts: "The climb is too steep." "That summit is unreachable by me." "I can worship just the same here at the base without all that 'extra stuff.'" "Climbing makes me uncomfortable, and God wouldn't call me to be uncomfortable." But as Pope Benedict XVI so eloquently reminded us, "The world promises you comfort, but you were *not made for comfort. You were made for greatness.*"[2]

A shorter Mass would be much easier, yes. Think of how much more comfortable the padded rocking-chair, theater-style seating would be rather than wooden pews and worn-out kneelers. Think of the money our Catholic churches could bring in if each one had a Starbucks in the vestibule, like some of our Protestant friends. Are we just clueless to the needs of the flock or the ways of the world? Has the modern age just passed right by our little universal Church of one billion souls? Or is there something more to what we're doing?

Now, this is not to say that non-Catholic forms of worship are bad or empty or fruitless, not at all. We can learn a great deal from our Protestant brothers and sisters, and they from us. We must always seek, first, the kingdom of God (Matthew 6:33) and build on our common ground of Jesus Christ. As Catholics, however, we believe that the Mass is a foretaste of heaven, the most intimate physical encounter of Christ imaginable. This *is* the kingdom of heaven, made available to us on earth, strengthening us for our journey home, a journey that is often treacherous.

> As Catholics, we believe that the Mass is a foretaste of heaven.

Just as with the sabbath rest we discussed in the last chapter, God doesn't will us to rest or invite us into communion with him because *he* needs it but because *we* do. And since worship is his idea, it follows rationally (like all things in the Christian life) that we ought to seek what God's will is for us when it comes to worshipping him and not merely seek the simplest or the most entertaining path with the least resistance. It's not about our comfort; it's about our greatness, which is achieved through our sanctity.

The richest and most comfortable people might get hailed and envied on earth, but it's the holiest and most humble whose names echo with greatness in the halls of heaven. The valley doesn't afford us the same perspective as the summit. The closer we get to heaven, the more different earth begins to look.

Piles of Rocks, Hearts of Stone

A Catholic priest and a nondenominational pastor were strolling through a park one day, discussing and debating theology and philosophy, life and ministry. The priest spoke about his love for the Mass, but the pastor was puzzled. Why spend so much on architecture and art, which only distract? Why all the ritual? What's the purpose, when so many Catholics seem so uninvolved and fail to even sing or give financially?

The priest acknowledged many of the problems that Catholics face. Still, he said, "Where do you think we learned the formula for worship? It's in the Bible, my friend. We worship God in the way he asks us to worship him."

The Mass is God's desired form of worship. The Mass is not our idea but God's. We didn't make this up; God did. We aren't the ones doing the work; God is the one who does it. It's about God, not us. He does the heavy lifting.

To gain a better understanding of this idea, let's go back in time again. We're at the base of Mount Sinai. The temperature is hot enough to melt gold. The Israelite women and children are removing their earrings and gold pieces and bringing them to Aaron, who is fashioning them into a molten calf of gold. The people have grown tired of waiting on Moses and, by extension, the one true God.

A few months earlier, God had freed the Israelites from hundreds of years of slavery at the hands of the Egyptians. He raised up Moses and empowered him and his brother, Aaron (a priest), with a message. God sent plagues to demonstrate his celestial power over all of the false gods of Egypt. Again and again, the God of the Israelites showed the might of his hand against the Egyptian empire. He rained down fire to stop their chariots and parted the Red Sea into walls of water so that his children might emerge unscathed. Three months later, as Moses led his people to the base of Mount Sinai, the Lord God bid them to wash and prepare themselves for a great "theophany" (from the Latin, meaning "God shows"). It was to be a visible manifestation and encounter between God and his children, one so sacred that ceremonial washing and preparation were required (Exodus 19:10-11).

On the third day following the ceremonial preparations, there were peals of thunder and claps of lightning. The sound of a great trumpet blast wailed around the mountain as a thick cloud descended upon it. The people were warned not to ascend the mountain but to wait on the Lord. Most knew that it was at this time that the Lord had entrusted Moses with the Ten Commandments (Exodus 20). It's in the following chapters of Exodus, however, that we are given incredibly important insight into God's plan of worship.

God was giving Moses necessary warnings against worshipping false gods, instructions regarding the building of altars, and prescriptions for sacrifice to him. God gave Moses laws governing morality and society, entrusting him to make the people aware of what was admissible and egregious in his heavenly sight. Everyone seemed to be on the same page, or so Moses thought. When he ascended Sinai again, a cloud covered the mountain. Scripture describes it this way:

> The LORD said to Moses, "Come up to me on the mountain, and wait there; and I will give you the tables of stone, with the law and the commandment, which I have written for their instruction." So Moses rose with his servant Joshua, and Moses went up into the mountain of God. And he said to the elders, "Tarry here for us, until we come to you again; and, behold, Aaron and Hur are with you; whoever has a cause, let him go to them."

> Then Moses went up on the mountain, and the cloud covered the mountain. The glory of the LORD settled on Mount Sinai, and the cloud covered it six days; and on the seventh day he called to Moses out of the midst of the cloud. Now the appearance of the glory of the LORD was like a devouring fire on the top of the mountain in the sight of the people of Israel. And Moses entered the cloud, and went up on the mountain. And Moses was on the mountain forty days and forty nights. (Exodus 24:12-18)

In the forty days that followed, Moses would meet with God privately. But the Israelites' patience was growing thin. "What now?" they thought, wondering how long God would keep them waiting. Sure, he had rescued them from their Egyptian slave drivers, but that was *so last year* (about five months earlier, actually). What had God done for them lately? So they went to Moses' brother, Aaron, who was left in charge (Exodus 24:14), and as we still see prevalent some thirty-two hundred years later, popular opinion replaced unpopular truth.

The Israelites had been enslaved for hundreds of years, mind you. They had adopted Egyptian forms of worship and pagan rituals. In the midst of their slavery, they began to doubt God's fidelity and promises. That doubt led to mistrust and, eventually, an identity crisis. Unable to "see" their God, and beginning to doubt in his love for them, they turned to the idol worship so popular and prevalent with their Egyptian captors. They, like Adam and Eve before them and billions after them, forsook the Creator in favor of his creation. Vainglory robs us of true glory, as we saw in Eden, beneath Sinai, and in just about every conceivable corner of God's creation, when sin is our entrée of choice.

God knew well that his children's hearts had grown hardened in Egypt. The very first thing he commanded Moses to do was to lead his people into the desert . . . to do what? To worship him. God freed his people from bondage and slavery, yes, but that was only step one. He had taken the Israelites out of Egypt but step two of the plan—being unveiled with the covenant at Mount Sinai—was to *take Egypt out of the Israelites*. God knew what they needed, but his children were more focused on what they wanted.

> God knew what they needed, but his children were more focused on what they wanted.

At this point, God's children shortsightedly threw the One who freed them to the wayside in favor of their all-new, shiny, and "available" god (the golden calf) who would never call them out of their sin (since idols have a difficult time with conversation). While they were digging themselves a spiritual grave, Moses was receiving some timeless instruction that is still gracing us at Mass today. God was telling Moses how to build a sanctuary for worship and what he wanted included in it. God was giving Moses a shopping list of materials for the finest materials: gold, silver, bronze, silk, rams' skins, fragrant oils, and incense . . . all to be contributed from his people. The sanctuary was designed very specifically not by Moses but by God. It would contain lampstands and tapestries, walls and veils, an altar table and priestly vestments (Exodus 25–28). There would be incense and a laver bowl so that the one offering sacrifice could wash his hands first (Exodus 30). There was even a command to have enough oil so that a lamp could burn perpetually in the sanctuary (27:20-21). These were the prescriptions being given *by* God *to* Moses *for* the people.

Does any of this sound vaguely familiar to a Mass-going Catholic?

Altar-ed Vision

Our road to Easter Sunday moves through Holy Thursday and Good Friday. God calls us to nourish ourselves *daily* with him as our bread and sustenance (Matthew 6:11). This regular dependence speaks not only to praise but to worship; it speaks to an intimacy that God desires to have with us. At the same time, he reminds us of the need to take up our crosses *daily* (Luke 9:23) and follow him, reminding us that a true relationship of love will be steeped in sacrifice. And that is what separates the mountaintop experience from the valley below. Both places in the Exodus story had an altar, but only one was a sanctuary directed to God.

Have you ever stopped to consider why an altar is still so important to what we do as Catholics? Wouldn't a multipurpose table be more functional? Some of the Reformers asked that question many centuries ago. It's a valid question. If it is just a memorial meal, why would we need an altar?

It's not just about the sacrifice upon the altar, however; it's about the heart behind the sacrifice. Where does the priest stand when he looks out at the congregation and says, "The Lord be with you. . . . Lift up your hearts. . . . Let us give thanks to the Lord our God." That's right; he's standing behind an altar, offering a sacrifice, bidding us to give thanks and to offer not just bread and wine but our very lives and bodies back to God (Romans 12:1-2). The bread and wine are the easy part. God wants more.

Giving God Your Best

Following the fall, Adam and Eve's family grew, along with their problems. Soon after the glorious birth of their sons, we hear of humanity's first sibling rivalry and, eventually, its first homicide. Cain and Abel's story is famous in Scripture, but it's often misunderstood. It starts out simply enough. Adam and Eve have two sons, Cain and Abel. Together the family works on a farm; Cain tends to the crops while Abel tends to the animals. Then they decide to make a sacrifice to God. Scripture depicts it in this way:

> In the course of time Cain brought to the LORD an offering of the fruit of the ground, and Abel brought of the firstlings of his flock and of their fat portions. (Genesis 4:3-4)

It's at this point that we should ask the question, "Why?" as in, "Why did Cain and Abel bring an offering to the Lord in the first place?" Even if Abel were just following his older brother's move, what within Cain prompted him to do that? He's a farmer; he's not trying to scale some corporate ladder. He's not looking for more work to do. So what are we to learn from this story? Why would Cain even go to the trouble (though he didn't go to much) to offer something to God? Perhaps God had instructed him to do so. Perhaps it was intuitive on Cain's part, since the family obviously had a relationship with God. Consider the "why" of the sacrifice as you continue reading.

> And the LORD had regard for Abel and his offering, but for Cain and his offering he had no regard. So Cain was very angry, and his countenance fell. The LORD said to Cain, "Why are you angry, and why has your countenance fallen? If you do well, will you not be accepted?" (Genesis 4:4-7)

So Cain and Abel both offer a sacrifice to God, but God's reaction isn't the same to each brother. A clue is hidden in verses 4 and 5 as to why God liked Abel's sacrifice so much more than his older brother's: Abel gave God the best animals that he had. The word "firstling" means the first crop or first animal of a season, which also means the best crop or best animal of that season. The Scripture verse does not make a distinction like that about Cain's fruit offering. It's as if Abel went out into the herd of animals and found the absolute best to sacrifice, while Cain just grabbed whatever fruit was lying around (possibly bruised or rotting) and let that be his sacrifice. Imagine how good Abel's sacrifice must have been for such a distinction. It must have been the biggest, fattest, juiciest Grade-A steak this world has ever seen for God to have been so wowed by Abel's sacrifice. Obviously, Cain's "sacrifice" must have paled in comparison, sort of like the juicy hamburger versus a tiny garnish, right? Well, not exactly.

Yes, it does say that the offering was Abel's best, but what pleased God wasn't so much Abel's animals but Abel's *attitude*. Notice that verse 5 says "*but for Cain and his offering* [God] had no regard" (emphasis added). So it wasn't necessarily the crop that God was displeased with; God was displeased with Cain. Something was wrong with Cain's attitude or within Cain's heart.

God even gives Cain another chance, explaining that if he offered a better sacrifice, he, too, would be held in high regard (Genesis 4:7). Before we move on, though, it's important to note something here. God's love for Cain was not based on his performance. God's love is not about "what you do"; he loves you for who you are. Cain's lackluster sacrifice didn't mean that God loved Cain less; it meant that God was disappointed because Cain didn't love God more. He wanted to help Cain understand what true love requires: it requires *sacrifice*. When we sacrifice, we show our love by putting others before ourselves.

You most likely know how the story turns out. Cain becomes so filled with rage that he lures his brother and then murders him in the field. The black sheep overpowers the white sheep, and the Shepherd is furious. Cain is then exiled, and with that, he got what he wanted. Cain desired to be first, not last, and would no longer have to "keep up" with young Abel. So there Cain went, alone, ashamed, and awfully miserable.

Why Sacrifice to God?

Let's get back to the original question of the "why" behind the sacrifice, because the Catholic Mass, first and foremost, is a sacrifice.

Have you ever wondered why we sacrifice things to God in the first place? Why would God want us to sacrifice to him? When God asks us, his creation, for a sacrifice, like an animal in Abel's case, it's not because he needs it. God doesn't need food; every-thing is his anyway. Since he is the Creator of all things, it means that absolutely everything we have is a gift from him: every drop of rain, blade of grass, piece of fruit, every animal and person.

God ask us to sacrifice because we need it.

God ask us to sacrifice because we need it. We, as his cre-ation, need to remember whom our blessings come from. We need to show the Creator that we love him more than his cre-ation. By sacrificing things back to him, we show that we not only rely on God, but also that we are more in love with the One who gives us the blessings than we are with the blessings themselves.

As Cain was reminded, there is nothing you can do to make God love you more. And there is nothing you can do to make God love you less. God loves us perfectly. Going to church doesn't make God love you more. Rather, going to church helps us to love God and our brothers and sisters in Christ more. Praising God doesn't make God love you more. Rather, praising God helps us to focus less on ourselves and more on God. Serving the poor, giving money to the Church, resisting temptation and sin, fasting, or making other sacrifices doesn't make God love you more. But it does please him, since all of those efforts and small sacrifices help us to grow in love and become more like Christ.

Sacrifice is one of the most basic of human actions and needs. In sacrificing something to God, we reaffirm who he is and who we are not. We demonstrate that God is greater than we are and that all good gifts come from him. Since everything we have is ultimately a gift from God (except sin—that's all ours), we honor God by offering our gifts back to him through a sacrifice.

Back down the Mountain

What do you sacrifice for this mountaintop experience of Mass? When have you gone out of your way or rearranged your schedule to improve the quality of the liturgy, for instance? Have you put your musical talents at the service of the Lord and his people (1 Peter 4:10)? Have you offered to lector or serve as an extraordinary minister of the Eucharist? How about volunteering to be a hospitality minister greeting people on the way in or helping out with refreshments and gatherings following Mass?

What are you sacrificing each week in order to get to Mass? What are you moving, shifting, or eliminating from your calendar so that the Mass and the Sabbath are truly primary? What prayers and intentions are you bringing with you? Are you exiting the door lamenting how "bad" the liturgy is, or are you thanking God that you are able to go to Mass every Sunday? There are countless people in our world who would do anything to have Mass every week.

The answers to these questions keep Mass from becoming "just something we're supposed to do" and transform it into something we cannot live without. This is not merely the faith of our grandparents. It is our faith, where the religion of the past is forever made present for future generations to behold.

Questions for Reflection and Discussion

1. Why would God prescribe for his children to worship in a particular way? What is the Lord trying to teach us?

2. When you go to Mass, do you give the Lord the "first fruits" of your time, attention, and love? How might the idea of offering yourself as a sacrifice to God during the liturgy help you to get more out of Mass?

3. Why is the concept of sacrifice so difficult for us? Where in your life do you struggle with making sacrifices?

4. What sacrifice have you made to God lately? What motivated you to do so? Did you expect anything from the Lord as a result?

CHAPTER FOUR

Past Is Present:
Understanding Tradition

Holy Communion is the shortest and
safest way to heaven.
—St. Pius X

For God so loved that world . . . that he gave us college football.

As a cradle-Catholic kid from the Midwest raised to love the "Fightin' Irish" of Notre Dame, there was little more that mattered at our house on Saturdays in the fall. We were a Notre Dame family—my father and uncles were alumni, and my mother and aunts had attended St. Mary's College, right across the street. So it wouldn't surprise you to hear that the mobile in my crib played the fight song.

The campus of Notre Dame in South Bend, Indiana, is a gorgeous blend of antiquity and modernity. Whether you enter the library, the golden dome, or the grotto, you walk where legends tread. While I'd love to say that most tourists consider the basilica on campus the most sacred space, it often (sadly) takes a distant second to the famed Notre Dame football stadium, "the house that Rockne built." The football field, the locker room, the famed tunnel where players exit to take the field of battle—these are historic landmarks that stand as symbols of past greatness and future hope for championships to come.

Whether you root for Mary's Irish or your own hometown team, watching college football on Saturdays is about life and tradition. A true fan of the game understands that Saturdays are about far more than the sixty minutes of action on the field. For a student of the game, every play has significance. For alumni, every tradition is held dear. The meaning and "reverence" shown toward the entire Saturday spectacle are directly proportional to ones's upbringing, allegiance, interest, and personal passion.

So that's Saturday. But what about Sunday?

Arrows toward Heaven

In college football, there are various elements that bring the game to life and transform it from just an athletic competition into something greater: a true celebration. Bands and cheerleaders, mascots and fight songs, cheers and traditions, tailgaters and victory parties—they all work together to "elevate" the game. These elements are obvious, discernible to the naked eye on any number of campuses across the land. They signify and point toward something greater than themselves. These elements, taken together, call our attention to a larger collective reality.

Consider now some of the visible elements within the Catholic liturgy. The stained glass and the statues, the candles and the tapestries, the incense and the bells, the holy water and the kneelers—all are arrows that do more than remind us; they point us to heaven opening up before us. They all speak to something greater than themselves, where form and function merge in a sacramental meaning often lost on the average Mass-goer. But it doesn't stop there. The music and silence, the chants and responses, the procession and genuflection, the proclamations and elevations, the consecration and communion all invite and encourage a response on our part. These are not mere movements within a ritual; these are moments of divine inspiration, encounters with the living God. This is nothing short of a front-row seat in the throne room of heaven!

At Mass we show up physically (and, we hope, spiritually) prepared, and we wait on God to do "his part." We schedule the servers and order the bread and wine. We dress the altar and

> God does the work, inviting us to behold the mystery.

arrange the music. We practice the readings and pass the baskets. We light the candles and set out the vessels. We bring our humanity and lay it down in the face of God's divinity, trusting that he will transform us the way he transforms the elements of bread and wine, taking all that is us and leaving us his very self in return (2 Corinthians 5:15; Galatians 2:20). Another ordinary Sunday offers an extraordinary opportunity for intimacy of communion, everlasting life, and true sainthood.

Just as we see in the Bible, we show up and set the stage, and God does the work, inviting us to behold the mystery.

Setting the Stage

The land was parched and arid. For three years they had waited for water, but the drought showed no signs of letting up. Under the rule of King Ahab, all of God's prophets had been cut down at the order of his wicked wife, Jezebel. Only one prophet was left standing to oppose the evil couple, and his name was Elijah.

God sent his mighty mouthpiece to King Ahab with a challenge. Elijah was commanded to seek the king's false prophets for a high-noon showdown on Mount Carmel. Not only was Elijah challenging the 450 false prophets of Baal, but also the 400 prophets of Asherah (1 Kings 18:19). That's 850 prophets against little ol' Elijah, atop the mountain, with the whole of Israel witnessing the sacrificial insanity from down below.

It was at this point, in the early morning hours, that Elijah set the "terms" of the competition between his God and the god named Baal. Elijah said:

Let two bulls be given to us; and let them choose one bull for themselves, and cut it in pieces and lay it on the wood, but put no fire to it; and I will prepare the other bull and lay it on the wood, and put no fire to it. And you call on the name of your god and I will call on the name of the LORD and the God who answers by fire, he is God." And all the people answered, "It is well spoken." Then Elijah said to the prophets of Baal, "Choose for yourselves one bull and prepare it first, for you are many; and call on the name of your god, but put no fire to it." And they took the bull which was given them, and they prepared it, and called on the name of Baal from morning until noon, saying, "O Baal, answer us!" But there was no voice, and no one answered. And they limped about the altar which they had made. (1 Kings 18:23-26)

So the prophet Elijah set the terms, the stage, and the altar. The prophets of Baal had a bull; Elijah had a bull. They had an altar; Elijah had an altar. They called on their god . . . and nothing. For hours, the false prophets prayed that their god would rain down fire from heaven . . . and *nada*. My favorite part of the story, however, occurs in the verses that follow, when the mighty prophet Elijah makes use of "holy sarcasm." With their sacrifice untouched after literally hours of beseeching their god, Baal, Elijah decides to offer some constructive criticism and oh-so-helpful advice.

> And at noon Elijah mocked them, saying, "Cry aloud, for he is a god; either he is musing, or he has gone aside, or he is on a journey, or perhaps he is asleep and must be awakened." . . . And as midday passed, they raved on until the time of the offering of the oblation, but there was no voice; no one answered, no one heeded. (1 Kings 18:27, 29)

Did you catch that? Here stands Elijah, surrounded by 850 false prophets, with the whole of Israel looking on, and so brazen is the prophet that he begins goading them. This is more than a display of guts or even stupidity on Elijah's part; this is akin to Elijah's signing his own death warrant. Queen Jezebel had already made sure that the rest of the prophets of the one true God had been murdered. Nothing would prevent Elijah from becoming the last and greatest casualty except for one thing—fire from heaven. If God failed to respond, as Baal had failed to do, Elijah would be up a dry river creek with no paddle, no boat, and no hope. Then, as if the odds were not stacked against him enough, Elijah decides to go even further in demonstrating the mighty power of God atop the mountain.

He drenches the altar with water—so much water that it fills the three-gallon trench surrounding it. He drenches it again and then a third time. That bull is saturated, as is the wood. No amount of lighter fluid will get this barbecue going. Then Elijah prays, and the heavens open and the fire falls. The flames enter the sanctuary made by human hands, and when God is finished, nothing is left, not even the stones or the water. The onlookers, filled with awe, kneel prostrate in worship of the one true God. As for the false prophets, they don't just lose face; they lose their lives that day (1 Kings 18:30-39).

Notice that Elijah merely set the stage. He followed God's command to assemble the people of Israel and called them to Mount Carmel. He prepared the altar, the offering, and his heart for sacrifice. When the time came, though, it wasn't his power that brought heaven's fiery fury; it was his prayer. Elijah did nothing more than prepare a way for God's glory and power to be made manifest. He used worldly elements to unleash heavenly realities; Elijah did his part so that God could do his. The sacrifice and the altar were prepared by human hands, but the sacrifice was transformed by heaven's. The earthly was consumed by the ethereal.

In Elijah's example of fidelity, we learn many things about trusting in God, about our smallness even amid perceived greatness, and about the need for total reliance on the Lord at every stage of our lives. Elijah's is the posture we ought to carry with us into the church for Mass, mighty only because of God's life within us. Like Elijah, we should arrive for our mountaintop experience because we were called by God to do so. We prepare the gifts and our hearts and offer them both on an altar of sacrifice to the Lord. Faced with the problem of evil and eventual death, we turn to our Lord—and our Lord alone—as our source of life, our protector, and our Savior. We turn our eyes to heaven, offering our miniscule sacrifice with total surrender and trust. The awesome reality of the

> God accepts our offer of ourselves and comes to make his home in us.

Eucharist is that we sinners, because of his great mercy, are able to consume the God of the universe. And even more awesome is that God accepts our offer of ourselves and comes to make his home in us.

Where was Elijah standing when he called down the fire of heaven to consume the sacrifice before the assembly of the people? That's right, at an altar. Have you ever noticed that part of Mass when the priest extends his hands over the bread and wine upon the altar and brings them down in a sort of drawn-out, sweeping motion? That liturgical moment, signified by the blessing gesture, is called the *epiclesis* (Greek for "calling down"). We Catholics love our big words, especially from the Latin or Greek, but every movement within the Mass is significant. The priest doesn't make that gesture sitting in his chair. No, when the priest calls down the Spirit of God to transform the sacrifice, where does he stand? Like Elijah almost three thousand years before him, the priest stands at an altar, built on twelve (apostolic) stones.

Clues within the Mystery

As was previously mentioned, creation is like one huge arrow pointing to the Creator. A wedding ring symbolizes and speaks to a far greater reality than just the gold; it points to the love of a married couple. A flag flown at half-mast is a stark and grave reminder that an influential soul was lost or that a great tragedy has befallen a country. Certain symbols carry meaning well beyond their cloth or precious metal. They redirect our hearts and minds to something greater and more meaningful.

The Catholic Mass is no different. It is the greatest of all creation's arrows pointing us to heaven because it invites us into heaven itself. More than just a sign or symbol, it is the pre-eminent sacrament from which all others draw their enduring power—the boundless love and mercy of God made present to us in the humblest of forms. The Mass is a cataclysmic event because it is the intermingling of heaven and earth, where all things visible point to the invisible and all things meaningful represent realities of even greater meaning. The liturgy is heavenly but is made known to us on earth through perceptible signs.

Just as a major motion picture requires writers, directors, producers, designers, and actors to make the drama unfold, so does the Mass require certain elements and people to come together to make good liturgy happen. Much like Elijah atop the mountain, the Mass requires that we put our gifts and talents into the hands of God, allowing him to take something simple and transform it into something majestic.

God has always been the Master of doing a lot with very little: five loaves and two fish (John 6:9-13); a rib (Genesis 2:22); five smooth stones (1 Samuel 17:40-52); the jawbone of an ass (Judges 15:15-17); a handful of flour and some oil in a jug (1 Kings 17:12-14); some spit (John 9:6-11); a shadow (Acts 5:15). God doesn't need much to radically change peoples' lives forever. He still does a lot with a little. At Mass, Christ is not only present but the one doing all the work. Jesus is the one doing the "heavy lifting," even if his "yoke is easy and his burden light" (cf. Matthew 11:30).

When we hear that Christ is "present" in the liturgy, we are not saying he is present as you and I in the pews are present. No, it's far deeper than that. We encounter Christ principally in four places at every single Mass. First, we see Christ in the community gathered. By virtue of our baptism, Christ is very much alive in each one of us through the power of the Holy Spirit. Next, we encounter Christ in the person of the priest. The priesthood of the new covenant—Christ's priesthood—is blessedly unique (but we'll deal with that in the next chapter). Third, we hear and experience him in the Sacred Scriptures. Not only do we have the four readings proclaimed, but almost every prayer and response throughout Mass comes directly out of the Bible. Finally and most important, we encounter God uniquely and completely in his Eucharistic Body and Blood. Far more than a symbol, the Eucharist is the fullness of God's life, his very body, blood, soul, and divinity made present and available to us upon that altar.

These are powerful realities and high mystery. These four encounters with God don't work in unison anywhere else in creation outside the Catholic liturgy. To be sure that we comprehend this incomprehensible truth, the Lord, by way of his Church on earth, has filled the Mass with symbols and markers that signify what is transpiring every step of the liturgical way.

Understanding the Physical Elements

The Mass is made up of movements and content. There is a cast of characters—lectors, musicians, altar servers, cantors—coming together to put their gifts and talents at the service of the Lord. Each character functions within this "backdrop" of the church and sanctuary. Before we get to the "script" of the Mass, however, it's essential to talk about the "set"—the physical elements.

Think of all the physical elements that you see or find in every Catholic church, regardless of the diocese or continent you're standing in: candles, an altar, incense, communion wafers, altar linens, white "purificators" for cleaning the chalices, the red candle beside the tabernacle, and the purple, green, white, or red for each liturgical season. Why go to all the trouble? Why not just scale it down and ease back a bit and save a whole bunch of people a whole lot of work? Is it just the Catholic Church being ritualistic for the sake of man-made traditions?

Of course not. There is larger, deeper realites at work in our liturgies, but if we don't understand them, it's easy to begin believing that we cling to these traditions out of fear rather than from God-inspired awe. The truth is that with each and every one of these sacramental elements, the Church is trying to teach us something—and point us toward Someone.

Priestly Vestments

You won't ever see a priest shopping at the grocery store in his chasuble or, for that matter, a priest saying Sunday Mass at the parish wearing khakis and a polo shirt. That's because the vestments signify something important. Just as the priests of the Old Testament wore liturgical vestments when offering sacrifices in the Temple, so the priest's liturgical dress today is meaningful, steeped in history but linking us to the present.

The alb, derived from *albus* (the Latin word for "white"), has been in common use as a liturgical garment since the latter part of the fourth century. The original symbolism was a direct reference to the seamless white garment that Christ wore during his passion. Furthermore, it has always been used as a means to remind the liturgical celebrant that his role at that moment is *in persona Christi* ("in the person of Christ"). As the priest takes the white garment and very simply covers his daily clothing, the vestment reminds him that he is no longer acting on his own accord.

The chasuble (from the Latin for "hooded cloak") is the colored sleeveless garment worn over the alb. The chasuble's color varies according to the liturgical season or feast day and is designed not as a fashion statement but as a statement of office and of function as celebrant of the Mass. The chasuble is also intended to be a sign of the priest's charity. Interestingly, the stole the priest wears (the long strip of fabric he puts around his neck that hangs down off both shoulders) is a sign of his priestly authority. When the chasuble is placed *over* the stole, it's a reminder that as important as his authority is, it must be overshadowed and covered in love.

For many centuries, the vesting ritual that the priest would go through prior to a liturgy was very precise, as each garment carried with it a spoken prayer. The particular prayer reminded the priest to put away whatever worldly cares or worries that he was carrying with him, better enabling him to meet the spiritual needs of his people and allowing him to become a *tabula rasa*—a "blank slate"—upon which the prayers and intentions of his congregation could be written.

A deacon wears an alb during the liturgy as well, but his stole is normally worn more as a sash, draping from the left shoulder and joined on the right waist. This differentiation shows that while deacons share in the priestly office in a unique and important way, their role is differentiated from that of priests.

Sacramentals and Symbols

Crucifixes, candles, incense, holy water, and statues are all examples of Catholic sacramentals and symbols. These elements are designed to illuminate our senses and draw us back to the worship of our God. Some elements, like candles and incense, began with practical purposes (for light or to mask smells) when the Mass was being said in less than ideal locations at the time of the early Church. Over time, the symbolic meaning of each overtook their practical necessity.

It might be helpful to take a "tour" of your local parish and spend some time in every part of the church. You could pray with the saints whose images are emblazoned upon the stained glass and captured by the wood and plaster of statues. Gaze upon the crucifix. Recommit yourself to your baptismal vows, and thank God for the gift of your relationship every time your fingers hit that holy water. During Mass, lean into the liturgy, and contemplate the ways in which each and every one of these elements is designed to captivate your senses and draw you further into the mystery of the Mass.

Altar

As we've already seen, the Mass is a sacrifice. Throughout the Old Testament, our patriarchs, including Abraham, Isaac, Jacob, Moses, Joshua, and David, built altars to God to offer their sacrifices and their very lives. We not only place our gifts of bread and wine upon it or our alms before it, but we are also invited to spiritually place our whole selves, with all our hopes and fears.

It's interesting to note that many churches are built in the cruciform (the form of the cross), lengthwise with short "arms" jetting out to the sides of the sanctuary. The architecture points us to Christ's body upon the cross and to the sanctuary. The sanctuary is located where our Lord's heart would be, and from the sanctuary at every Mass, blood and water flow to bring life to his Church.

Ambo

The elevated lectern gives visible prominence to the word of God. In the early days, the raised ambo (from medieval Greek for "pulpit") offered better projection and acoustics to the faithful gathered together. In the days of modern sound systems, the ambo is not quite as raised as it once was, but it still functions as a station set apart from the altar but within the sanctuary, from which the timeless truths of God are to be shared.

Lectors are liturgical ministers at Mass and ought to take their service every bit as seriously as extraordinary ministers of the Eucharist. They should take great care to practice the readings, pronounce the words correctly, and project their voices so that they are heard. The word of God deserves our highest reverence, which is why the Book of the Gospels is elevated during the procession into the church and during the recession on the way out. It is also why the priest or deacon often elevates it and even kisses it before proclaiming the Gospel reading.

Posture

Standing, sitting, kneeling, bowing (slight or profound), and genuflecting all communicate something different at the various moments of the Mass. Why do we do which, and when? The more mindful we become about what each action signifies and when it transpires, the more clues we will have as to what is happening within each stage of this mystery we call the Mass.

> Kneeling is a profound symbol of adoration.

Prior to entering or exiting the pew, we genuflect (Latin for "on bended knee"), kneeling down on one knee as an outward sign of the interior posture of our hearts. Genuflection offers visible respect to the Lord, who is truly present within the tabernacle (Latin for "tent"), where the Eucharist, Christ's Body, is kept.

Kneeling is a profound symbol of adoration—not just bowing but falling on our knees before the King of the universe. Throughout Scripture, we see heroes and heroines falling prostrate to worship God, as the magi did in Bethlehem (Matthew 2:11) or Christ's disciples did in Simon Peter's boat following a mighty storm at sea (Matthew 14:33).

When the name of Jesus or the Blessed Virgin Mary is uttered, you may notice some offering a slight bow as a sign of adoration (Jesus) or veneration (Mary and the saints). When we head forward to receive Communion, however, a profound bow (at the waist) is encouraged. Some people prefer to genuflect before receiving the Eucharist as a sign of their reverence, which is allowed but often not encouraged (for reasons of liturgical flow during Communion and of safety).

During longer periods of the Mass, such as during the readings and the homily, we are encouraged to sit to maximize our comfort and attention span. At certain times within the Mass, we stand to demonstrate respect (such as when the priest enters or exits) or honor (while listening to the Gospels, because Christ is present in the word), or our willingness to act (such as during the Prayers of the Faithful, to do what we can to fulfill our intentions, or during the Gospels, to go out and proclaim the good news).

Vessels

If you were asked to find "ciborium," would you look on the periodic table of elements or within the sacristy (the room where the priest's vestments and sacred vessels are stored)? The ciborium (from the Latin *cibus* for "food") is the golden or silver bowl that holds the Eucharistic bread; the chalice (from the Latin *calix* for "cup") holds the Lord's most sacred Blood. Each and every vessel used within the Mass is blessed and should be made from the finest materials (gold or silver) because that is what the Lord and the liturgy deserve: our very best. They are to be cared for, cleaned, and used according to specifications that ensure reverence and not just functionality.

So for all of the often misunderstood "pomp and circumstance" that's associated with the Catholic liturgy, it's not necessarily complex. In fact, it's quite simple. Understanding the signs and symbols around us can enrich our experience of the Mass and help us to see beyond our earthly lenses.

The more we come to understand what is truly transpiring in church, most specifically in the sanctuary, the more we will be doing Monday through Saturday to prepare ourselves to receive all that the Lord wishes to give us. When we get frustrated because we don't "get much out of Mass," it's because we're looking at things through an earthly lens. When we bring a Dixie cup to Niagara Falls, we leave bewildered and parched. But if we knew the overflowing fountain of grace being poured out from the altar, we would be furiously working to find the biggest bucket we could bring.

And at that altar is the priest, standing in the person of Christ, offering to God on our behalf what we offer to him. We provide him with the elements: the bread, the wine, our alms, and our sin-tattered hearts, trusting that through the power of the liturgical sacrifice, the Spirit can breathe peace into our lives and life into our dry bones (Ezekiel 37) for another week of spiritual battle. The grace of the Mass is made available not by us but by Christ. The Most Blessed Sacrament, the Eucharist, is made present through the power of the Holy Spirit moving through the Catholic priesthood.

Put simply, without the priest, there is no Mass.

Questions for Reflection and Discussion

1. Why do you think God uses visible signs to communicate the invisible? Why do we need such signs?

2. What is one tradition or element within the Mass that you enjoy or that is especially meaningful to you personally? Why?

3. How often do you consider that you are encountering Christ in the people next to you in the pews, including your own family members? Why is this important to recognize?

4. What was one interesting "detail" or fact regarding the outward signs (i.e., vestments, sacramentals, etc.) that you had either forgotten or never learned before?

CHAPTER FIVE

The Original Men in Black: Understanding the Priesthood

Priests have received a power which God has given neither to angels nor to archangels.
—*St. John Chrysostom*

A priest was visiting Rome for an audience with then Pope John Paul II. On his way to the meeting, the priest stopped into a local Roman church to pray. Heading up the steps, he passed by some beggars looking for help. Moments later, upon entering the church and kneeling in prayer, the priest realized that he knew one of the beggars. He rushed back outside, looked the man in the eye, and said, "Don't I know you?" The beggar replied, "Yeah, we went to seminary together."

"So you're a priest, then?" he asked. The beggar retorted, "I used to be, but look at me now! I'm doing really well, huh? What do you think?"

In a hurry for his meeting with the pope, the priest assured the beggar that he'd pray for him, to which the poor man replied, "Lot of good that'll do."

During his meeting with the Holy Father, the priest could not stop thinking about his interaction with his former classmate. So overcome with sorrow was the priest that he apparently blurted out and recounted the entire story to the pope in the midst of their meeting.

Apparently, a few hours after their meeting, the priest received a phone call from the Vatican inviting both him and the beggar priest to dine with the pope that night. The priest went back and found the beggar, rented a room for him at a hotel, helped him get cleaned up and changed, and the two made their way to the pope's private residence. Following dinner and prior to dessert, the pope asked the priest to step out for a few moments so that he could speak privately with the beggar priest.

About twenty minutes later, the doors opened, and the priest was invited back in for dessert and conversation. Shortly thereafter, the two men thanked the Holy Father for his hospitality, said goodnight, and were on their way. Once outside, the priest, unable to hold his excitement, asked his beggar friend, "What happened? What did the pope say? Did he hear your confession?"

Overwhelmed with emotion and humility, the beggar spoke quietly and timidly through shaking lips. "No. The pope wanted me to hear his confession." Through tear-filled eyes the man continued, "I said, 'Me! How could I hear your confession? I am just a beggar now!' At that moment, the pope raised his chin, looked into my eyes, clasped my hands, and replied, 'So am I. We are all beggars before the Lord.'"[3]

Who Is the Priest?

Pope St. John Paul II had a great love and a deep understanding of the priesthood. One of the many documents he wrote was an apostolic exhortation entitled *Pastores Dabo Vobis* (translated "I Will Give You Shepherds"). It outlined not only what a priest *does* but, more to the point, who he is called to *be* by God and for the Church.

In sharing in Christ's priesthood, the priest's authority stems from his servanthood. John Paul writes that he must be "a man of communion" as well as "a man of mission and dialogue" (18). He must approach God's word "with a docile and prayerful heart so that it may deeply penetrate his thoughts

> The priesthood of Jesus Christ is rooted in deep mystery.

and feelings and bring about a new outlook in him—'the mind of Christ' [1 Corinthians 2:16]" (26). He must be a "concrete and joyful witness," with "not only his words, but his very presence" (39).

The priesthood of Jesus Christ is an exercise in self-mastery and is rooted in deep mystery. It is enigmatic and often misunderstood. It has both a practical and a mystical dimension—earthly in its demands and ethereal in its directives. And since no one but a priest can say Mass, it is essential that we understand better who the priest is before discussing what he does.

The Priest as Servant

On a typical corporate flowchart, the CEO would reign atop a series of executive-level positions. Below them are senior management, mid-level management, directors and supervisors, all the way down to the workers in the mail room and the unpaid pool of interns. Sadly, this is the way the Church's magisterial framework is normally viewed as well. People see the pope sitting as CEO, his cardinals as an executive-management team, and the bishops as senior management. Down the line are the priests, deacons, sisters, and, eventually, the low-paid or volunteer staffers in the "mail rooms" of parishes. This concept, however, is inherently myopic and even dangerous.

While the pope is the successor to St. Peter and the Vicar of Christ on earth, the earthly concepts of what constitutes a leader need to be altered for the men standing before our altars.

The priest is, first, a servant, not a parish CEO. The bishop, the priests' local "superior," has authority and responsibility but is still a *servant leader*. The cardinals and the pope, likewise, are called, first, to serve the needs of the people and to exercise their God-given authority to wash the feet of the Church. When the God of the universe took up the basin and towel in the upper room on that fateful Holy Thursday night, it was yet another sign that the priesthood of old was being transformed into something quite new.

The priests of the old covenant were set apart to offer sacrifice on behalf of the people. They donned long flowing robes. They offered their prayers aloud. They blessed and slaughtered the animals, drained their blood, and burned their carcasses. Their priesthood was sacrificial but external. It was an offering to the God "out there."

The priesthood was designed to bring the people to God and to bring God to the people. Over the centuries of nomadic tribes, slavery, desert wanderings, wars, famine, victories, kingdoms, devastation, exile, and rebuilding, seemingly the only constant we see in the Old Testament is God's presence and an ongoing priesthood. Through both the proverbial highs and lows of this journey of faith, God called priests to shepherd his people. Most were good. Many were bad (see Isaiah 56; Jeremiah 23; Ezekiel 34). God knew some would sin. God warned them, and us, that some would turn from him, yet God continued to call them.

So why call priests when a small percentage would violate their vocation? Put simply, because *we need them*. Where the priest goes, God's presence goes in a sacred and unique way.

> Where the priest goes, God's presence goes in a sacred and unique way.

That night of the Last Supper, Christ offered a tangible, visible example of what this "new" priesthood of his is going to look like. This is not a "Do as I say, not as I do" priesthood that Christ is embodying; instead, his words to "Do this in remembrance of me" is the embodiment par excellence. This priesthood that Christ created anew is rooted and inspired by Christ's own servant leadership. Christ's priesthood measures greatness not by miters and croziers but by blood, sweat, and tears, as we see in the bowels of Gethsemane, atop the rocks of Calvary, and within parishes and rectories across the globe. Priestly greatness is seen in holiness, and priestly leadership, through servitude.

The Priest as Sinner in Need of a Savior

St. John's eyewitness account of the events that transpired in the holy cenacle (Latin for "upper room") prior to the Passover meal

(John 13:1) offers God's children the final and necessary pieces to the Gospel puzzle. The washing of the feet, in a way, makes the Eucharistic sacrifice possible. This outward act of service humbles the heart and prepares the soul for the inner act of service that the Eucharist will catalyze. Our priests, before they can stand in the person of Christ, must allow themselves to be formed and transformed by him. Christ cleanses us—and the priest—of sin so that we can partake of his Body and Blood and become a part of him.

It's impossible to divorce the washing of the feet from the Eucharist, just as it is impossible to separate the Eucharist from the cross (which we'll get to next). You can't remove the foot washing from the Last Supper. The Gospels of Mark, Matthew, and Luke all include accounts of the consecration of Christ's body and blood during the Last Supper, which is lacking in John's account. And none of the synoptic Gospels include the foot washing. That doesn't mean that the beloved disciple, St. John, who penned his Gospel through the Spirit's inspiration, was just filling in random gaps of what happened that night. His story, in fact, is essential.

As the carpenter knelt and scrubbed the bloodied and calloused feet of his closest friends and students—feet that had followed him over hundreds of miles of ministry—each disciple's heart was forced to submit to this incomprehensible act of love. The God of the universe was performing an act of Mediterranean hospitality normally reserved for a slave. The King was bowing before his subjects in the most humbling way imaginable. So great was this act of love that Simon Peter even tried to stop Jesus. Three years earlier, Peter had been so overwhelmed by Christ's presence and mercy beside the Sea of

Galilee that he begged Jesus to depart from him. Now a storm began to rage on the sea of Simon's heart at the concept of the sinless One washing his sinful feet.

> He came to Simon Peter; and Peter said to him, "Lord, do you wash my feet?" Jesus answered him, "What I am doing you do not know now, but afterward you will understand." Peter said to him, "You shall never wash my feet." Jesus answered him, "If I do not wash you, you have no part in me." Simon Peter said to him, "Lord, not my feet only but also my hands and my head!" Jesus said to him, "He who has bathed does not need to wash, except for his feet, but he is clean all over; and you are clean, but not all of you." For he knew who was to betray him; that was why he said, "You are not all clean." (John 13:6-11)

Jesus' response is both startling and telling. If we aren't washed by him, we'll have no part *in him*. This is sacramental language, where we partake of him and he of us. In that moment it's clear that Peter (and the apostles) could not wholly comprehend what Jesus was saying, for they had yet to receive the Holy Spirit in its fullness. The Spirit, as we hear a little later in John's Gospel (John 16:13), will lead them into the fullness of truth and understanding.

Jesus' response to Simon Peter is not merely for Peter to recall later in a divinely inspired moment of retrospective reflection but for all of us down through the ages to contemplate. The response is so important that the Holy Spirit insisted that we'd have it from the pen of St. John. We *must submit* in humility to the great love of God. We *must* allow him to save us, to serve us, and (following the washing of the feet), *to feed us* if we want to truly live. This is true for both the priest and for us, the laity.

Only after the apostles had allowed Christ's mercy to wash over them externally could they begin to allow his grace and mercy to re-create them internally through his own body and blood. The feet, now clean, are a stunning visual representation of the need to approach the table of the Lord properly dressed (externally) and properly disposed (internally). Within Peter's response to Jesus' action, one can almost hear traces of the centurion a year before that we repeat at every single Mass: "Lord, I am not worthy to have you come under my roof" (Matthew 8:8). We say these words before we approach the table. They are an outward sign of our collective interior posture, an acknowledgement of God's greatness and our smallness, and a public profession that the only reason we can approach the throne of God's altar table is because he has invited and commanded us to do so (Hebrews 4:16; Matthew 26:26-28).

The Priest as the Sacrifice

As St. Jerome famously put it, "Ignorance of Scripture is ignorance of Christ." No truer statement has ever been uttered in regard to the importance of the Bible to the Christian. I'd submit, however, that as Catholic Christians, it is even more essential, for the more we "put out into the deep" (Luke 5:4) regarding the liturgy and its mystery, the more necessary it is to have Scripture as our vessel and the Holy Spirit as our wind. The greater our comprehension of Scripture, the more the Mass comes to life in our lives.

In the Catholic Mass, the Old and New Testaments intersect in powerful ways, as we've seen in the previous chapters.

The better we know the Bible, the more we will know what the movements and flow of the Mass mean and, assuredly, the more we will understand the purpose and vocation of our priests. Above all, the better we know Scripture, the more we will understand why the Catholic Mass is, first and foremost, a sacrifice.

> The better we know the Bible, the more we will know what the movements and flow of the Mass mean.

Our Mass in many ways resembles the Jewish Passover meal, in which the eldest male in the family would retell the story of the Israelites' exodus from the slavery and paganism of their Egyptian world. Only after the sharing of the story would the family partake in eating the paschal (Aramaic for "Passover") lamb. Recall in the second chapter how integral and important sacrifice is to us in our relationship with God. It's with that in mind that we turn our attention to his priests who, at Mass, participate in the once-and-for-all sacrifice of God that occurred in the upper room and upon Calvary's mount, for those two sacrifices are one. Jesus' sacrifice at the Last Supper and his sacrifice on the cross are, indeed, inseparable, two sides to the very same coin, and we see their unity in the title "Lamb of God." Before we move forward, however, we have to look backward, for the New Testament is hidden in the Old.

"Lamb of God" is one of the titles most commonly associated with Christ. We hear it in sacred music and art. It is the first title uttered by St. John the Baptist as our Lord approached the Jordan River (John 1:29). In that famous utterance, the Baptist gives us insight, not only into the meaning of the title, but also of Christ's purpose on earth: "The next day he saw Jesus coming toward him, and said, 'Behold, the Lamb of God, *who takes away the sin of the world!*'" (John 1:29, emphasis added).

Upon hearing that verse, many people may be confused, however, as to how exactly a lamb can take away sins. Christ's title as the "Lamb of God" points us not only to his mission but also to his identity. As was previously mentioned, through sacrifice we remain in "right order" with God, because it is a reminder of who we are before him. Additionally, though, sacrifice is used to set things right. As the Anglican bishop and Scripture scholar N.T. Wright has explained, "Sacrifice is the natural and appropriate human activity. . . . Sacrifice . . . lies deep within the human awareness that things which are wrong have to be put right; and the way in which they are put right involves the *conscience* and the *whole life* of those involved."[4] John the Baptist was calling for repentance and *metanoia*, a radical change of direction in one's life that leads to spiritual rebirth and renewal. So why the need for repentance, and what does the lamb have to do with it?

As I said earlier, to better understand the Catholic Mass, we must have a foundation in Sacred Scripture. Further, to better understand Scripture and our salvation history, it is helpful to view the stories of the Bible, both within the Old and New Testaments, through the lens of a *covenant* (as we discussed in the second chapter). The problem with broken covenants is that God's holiness demands justice. Since God is perfect justice and perfect love, he cannot just dismiss the covenant promise and consequence; if he did, he wouldn't fulfill his word, and that violates the very nature of God. On the other hand, he loved us too much to let us just die. God could not dismiss the sin, but God also did not want to dismiss us. We were left with a problem that only God could solve, and in Christ Jesus he did what we couldn't do. Jesus is the answer to our sinful past and our hopeless future.

A Story Too Important to Pass Over

During the tenth plague in Exodus, God prescribed a way for his people to be protected from death. He ordered every household to select a lamb, slaughter it, eat its flesh, and cover the wooden doorpost of their home with the lamb's blood. You can read about this in detail in Exodus 12. That night, the angel of death *passed over* the land of Egypt (that's where we get the term "Passover"), and in any home without the blood of the lamb upon its door, the firstborn male child died (12:29).

It's important to note here that animal sacrifice was quite commonplace in the ancient world, so God was using a well-known practice but reorienting it to himself (rather than to false gods). In commanding his people to spill the blood of these animals and then eat them, God made the gravest sin for the Egyptians (in this case) the path to freedom for his children, the Israelites. Recall, this is how God would "take Egypt out of the Israelites."

Long after the first Passover, God instituted a new tradition through his prophets. In Leviticus 16, God told Moses and Aaron the priest to select two goats for a sacrificial offering to atone for (meaning "to reconcile" or "make amends for") the sins of the people. The first goat was to be killed, and his blood was to be sprinkled on what was called the "mercy seat" on the ark of the covenant (which held the Ten Commandments). The blood was holy because it was seen as the source of life. When God saw the blood of the offering, he would remain merciful to his sinful children, and his forgiveness would be poured out upon them as they ate the animal's flesh. They were now in "communion" with the animal who had taken their place and paid their debt.

The priest would then lay hands on the second goat and confer the sins of the people on it. This goat (known as the scapegoat) would be allowed to live but would bear the sins of the people. He would be taken far into the wilderness and set free, and God would "remember their sins no more" (Jeremiah 31:43)).

Over time and following so many broken covenants, no animal sacrifice could cover the greatness of our sin any longer; our debt was too large and our sin, too great. So God himself took flesh through the Incarnation and did what we could never do by ourselves: cover our debt and save us from death. Jesus is the perfect and spotless lamb who was slain, the one who not only "covers" our debt of sin but who conquers sin and death (Romans 6:23; 1 Corinthians 15:21).

The Blood of the New Covenant

Consider now the Last Supper through this lens, and you find Jesus gathering his apostles on the feast of Passover, which commemorated the events of Exodus 12 described above. At that meal, Christ spoke of a new *covenant*:

Now as they were eating, Jesus took bread, and blessed, and broke it, and gave it to the disciples and said, "Take, eat; this is my body." And he took a cup, and when he had given thanks he gave it to them, saying, "Drink of it, all of you; for this is my blood of the covenant, which is poured out for many for the forgiveness of sins. (Matthew 26:26-28)

Here we see Christ as the Lamb of God, offering us his flesh to eat in the upper room on Holy Thursday night, when the apostles entered into communion with him in an extraordinarily new way. Each time we go to Mass, we are participating in Christ's once-and-for-all sacrifice two thousand years ago. The blood he shed on the cross (like the lamb's blood on the doorpost) saves us from death, and the flesh and blood we consume renews our covenant (but a new, eternal covenant) with him. At the original Passover, the Israelites were set free from the chains of slavery. Through the sacraments, still today, we are set free from sin and death and offered new life.

Obviously, the title "Lamb of God" carries with it great biblical history and significance. This is yet another example of how the Old Testament points to Jesus and how, in Christ and in the New Testament, the Old Testament takes on new meaning. The convergence of Old and New Testament readings at every Mass offers us more than a reminder of our ancestors and our "family tree." These covenants and events are the very roots of the tree, the foundation of most of our liturgical practices, and the reason why we enter into the sacrifice and consume the Lamb today.

At Mass, following the Liturgy of the Word, we recite the *Agnus Dei*, the "Lamb of God, who takes away the sin of the world" (John 1:29), twice asking the Lord to "have mercy on us" (*miserere nobis*) and once, to "grant us peace" (*dona nobis pacem*). For the priest, this title has special meaning. For if the priest is standing *in persona Christi* (in "the person of Christ") during Mass, offering a sacrifice to God the Father on our behalf, then he is not only the priest *offering* the sacrifice, but like Christ, who *is* the lamb, the priest must somehow become the lamb, become the sacrifice as well, as he offers our prayers to God on our behalf.

We hear echoes of this reality when the priest speaks the words of consecration. He is not merely quoting Scripture; he is speaking as Christ. When he takes, blesses, and breaks the bread, he doesn't say, "This is his Body" but, rather, "This is *my Body.*" Likewise, when he takes the chalice of wine, he invites us to drink not his blood but, in the words of Christ, "*my Blood,*" the blood of the new *covenant*. Do you see what's

> This is a special office, a unique vocation, a divine calling.

happening here? The priest isn't just the one offering the sacrifice *for* Christ; the priest is *sharing in and standing in* the priesthood of Christ. If the Mass were a mystery novel, the priest would be not only the detective solving the case; he would also be the victim! How's that for divine efficiency?

Not just anybody can do this. This is a special office, a unique vocation, a divine calling. It offers us much only after having required much. It's not easy being a priest.

A Good Priest Isn't Hard to Find

A good friend of mine is the pastor of a decent-sized suburban parish. He has a fairly competent parish staff, a handful of trustworthy and dependable volunteers, and great parishioners who, for the most part, love being Catholic. He also has unhealthy, unholy, and unrealistic expectations placed upon him daily.

Stop for a moment and ask yourself how a "good" priest is measured nowadays. One measure is by how entertaining or interesting his homilies are. He's expected to preach his very best homily three or four times a weekend, every single weekend. He is measured by his demeanor and attitude each and every moment of every day, regardless of how that day is actually going. He's sought for counsel yet measured oftentimes not by whether he has the "answer" but whether his answer—and, by extension, the Church's answer—agrees with someone's personal opinion. The priest is measured by whether he is "too Catholic" or "not Catholic enough." He's called on the carpet for his handling of every pothole and budget shortfall, every building project and maintenance issue within the parish, rectory, and parochial-school campus.

He's expected to be up early, on time and vested in the chapel for daily Mass even if he was called to the hospital in the middle of the night to administer the sacraments and anoint the sick. He's expected to be in the confessional when we decide to go and is held responsible if the line is too long for everyone to get in before Mass begins. He's supposed to remember every person's name, every fact about every saint, and the cross-reference for every major doctrinal teaching of the Church. He's also supposed to take care of himself, his own prayer life, his own rectory, and be responsible for any other brother priests in residence, seminarians who stay for the summer, and deacons who serve alongside him. Mind you, this is all before any of his responsibilities to the bishop on a diocesan level or for managing an often underpaid and overworked staff at the parish and parochial school.

Now as a father, I understand well that the proverbial buck stops with me, as do the pastors in our parishes. That being said, if it all falls on me, my family is going to fall apart. Families need to work together. I can make the dinner, but the kids have to help pull it together, set the table, and do the dishes. I can manage the budget, but others have to turn off the lights and be responsible with their things. I'm always called to be patient and kind, but some days I'm going to struggle with my temper more than others. I'm happy to offer counsel, help with homework, and settle disputes, but sometimes fulfilling my role as a father demands that I let my children work it out on their own, or else they won't learn.

In a similar way, the priest, although uniquely and mystically graced and blessed by God to fulfill his vocation, is father over a very large family and a complex home. He is called to handle every situation thrown his way by God, man, and the evil one with the highest virtue and class. We hold priests to a nearly impossible standard.

The reality is that if we are not praying daily for our priests, bishops, and the pope, we have missed Simon Peter's boat. If we have not yet gone to the Lord in thanksgiving for these men before complaining to the Lord about the lack of fish they're catching, we need to repent.

Prayer Changes Everything

As you can probably tell, I have a deep love for the priesthood of Jesus Christ. Likewise, I am consistently floored by the dedication and service of religious sisters and brothers. In my years of ministry, I have met amazing priests from all over the world. I am left speechless by their humble service and love. I've also never met such an incredibly overworked group of people in all my days. Some are overworked because it's a "season" that requires it. When the season ends, they find balance again. For others, the season never changes. Others are overworked because they fail to

> Christ left us his Eucharistic self and his mother to aid us in our weaknesses.

take their sabbath rest. They don't force the necessary separation between their ministry lives and their personal, spiritual lives. The two become one and the same, and the outcome is a well-intentioned soul burned out and fighting to keep his joy.

I've met many priests and religious who, in moments of total authenticity, have shared with me their personal struggle to pray. I've met even more who take on way too much at the parish because, in their own words, "There is no one else to do it." Similarly, I have met more holy priests than I can count who are really afraid to ask for help, fearing that such an image of humility will be taken advantage of, misinterpreted, or exploited. These are difficult issues, but they can be overcome. The truth is that Christ left us his Eucharistic self and his mother to aid us in our weaknesses. A priest's prayer life must come first, because prayer is more necessary than oxygen.

The best way for our priests (and religious) to keep their primary vocations primary is for them to be healthy spiritually, mentally, and physically. But they need our help to do it. The best thing we can do as laypeople, beyond prayer, to support our priests is to let them focus on being priests. Parishes, like homes, need many hands to keep them running. Stewardship of your own talents won't just build the kingdom; it will build up the parish and your priest. If you're handy, there are probably repairs you could do. If you're good with numbers, maybe you could serve on the parish finance team. If your gift is the ability to talk to people, I guarantee that Father would like to have your number in his cell phone for hospitality or fund-raising. Put simply, the more we take off Father's plate, the more time he'll have to "preach, teach, and sanctify," which is what he was ordained to do.

We need to do the smaller, "non-priestly" parish duties (or be empowered to do so), freeing up Father to pray more. Priests must remain disciplined in their prayer devotions, not falling into spiritual ruts but constantly letting Christ woo them again, constantly falling deeper in love with his most sacred heart in the Eucharist. Priests and religious also must constantly avail themselves of holy mental stimulation, first in the Sacred Scriptures *and only then* in the writings of the great saints or in other spiritual works. To any priests reading this, remember: the Bible cannot be your second choice. Beyond your breviary, dust off that Bible and read it daily anew. A worn-out Bible is the sign of a Catholic who is not.

One last thought about our priests. As mentioned previously, the most important thing the priest does is to administer the sacraments, but he is most often and most critically evaluated not for the prayer but for his preaching. In fairness, we've all been stuck in the pew when a priest's train of thought leaves the station, only to derail twenty minutes later in a mess of digression, forgotten points, or lost analogies. This is not to suggest that priests should not constantly strive to improve their teaching; they must. The gospel is designed to be heard—and lived, not merely read. Can you imagine, though, if your most consistent source of feedback and evaluation from the parish you love and were ordained to serve came back in the form of listless staring, yawning, rolling of the eyes, reading of the bulletin, or scribbling in a checkbook during your preaching? For many priests, the even sadder part is that often the only affirmation they receive as the faithful are hurriedly exiting the church after Mass is about a homily. What about gratitude for that priest's offering of his very self to make the God of the universe present and available to us upon the altar?

Commit to praying for your parish priest daily, and if you don't particularly connect with him or like him, pray for him twice as much. Make it a point to drop him a note thanking him for his priesthood and for who he is, not just for all he does. Affirm him frequently, to his face and to others. The pastor isn't just supposed to build up the parish; the parish is supposed to build up its pastor. Invite him over for dinner and to join your family in different settings and outings. He may decline, but at least the invitation is there and the thought put into action. Learn the anniversary day of his ordination and celebrate it. Do so for his birthday as well. Honor the man who gave his life to honor you. And finally, regardless of the length or quality of the preaching, try to lean in and listen for something that God is speaking to you through him. I've never heard a homily that I couldn't take at least one good point from, one pearl of great price or one golden nugget of wisdom that would serve me well to remember or employ in my daily life.

Questions for Reflection and Discussion

1. Have you ever thought of the priest standing in for Christ as the sacrifice? In what ways do you see your parish priest offering himself as a sacrifice to his parishioners?

2. What is the practical significance of Christ's washing of the feet? What is it supposed to remind us of on Monday through Saturday, in our homes, at the office, or in our neighborhood and parish community?

3. Is this image of Christ as the Lamb of God who takes away our sins something that enters your mind during Mass? How does this image bless your understanding of the sacrifice of the Mass?

4. In what ways do you support your parish priest or other priests whom you know? In what ways could you better support them?

CHAPTER SIX

For the Love of Family: Understanding True Community

The Church draws her life from the Eucharist.
—St. John Paul II

I don't think Noah gets enough credit. Here's a man who knew little about boatbuilding and, most likely, even less about animals. Nevertheless, God chose him to be a ship captain and amateur zookeeper. Noah's résumé didn't deem him worthy, but his heart did. When the rest of the world was seeking the world, Noah sought heaven.

Note that it wasn't just Noah whom God spared but his entire family: Noah, his unnamed wife (whom I like to call "Joan of Ark"), his three sons, and their three wives. These eight souls would live the inaugural season of reality television, part *Real World* and part *Survivor*, but without the benefit of cameras.

Noah the farmer was called under sunny skies to construct the world's first houseboat. Based upon the measurements for the craft, this was no weekend project—it wasn't going to be knocked out after a few trips to the local hardware store. No, God deemed exact measurements for the ark, and it was big: "This is how you are to make it: the length of the ark three hundred cubits, its breadth fifty cubits, and its height thirty cubits" (Genesis 6:15).

Noah's ark was basically the length of one and a half foot-ball fields, the width of almost two basketball courts, and as tall as a four-story building. Even with his three sons helping, this was a building project for the ages.

And to think that boatbuilding would turn out to be the easy part.

Then would come the gathering of animals. Children's books have romanticized the scene, and for good reason. Imagine the stench aboard that vessel. After forty days trapped inside during torrential rains, the Titanic would start to look attractive. After another hundred days on board with just your immediate family and every animal imaginable, you may have started to suspect that the truly blessed had been swept away in the flood (Genesis 7:24). Though it was the "getaway" of a lifetime, this was no family vacation. God wasn't trying to amuse Noah and his family. He was trying to save them, and salvation is messy.

Now consider the journey to Bethlehem and the flight to Egypt under the threat of a homicidal king. Recall the prophecy at Jesus' circumcision assuring Mary that she, too, would suffer. Remember the three days when the whereabouts of the boy Jesus was unknown to Mary and Joseph. How about Jesus' childhood neighbors from Nazareth getting ready to toss the carpenter-turned-prophet off the cliff? Think back to the Garden of Gethsemane, the "trial" before Caiaphas, the discourse with Pilate, and the scourging at the pillar. Contemplate the blood-covered rocks of Golgotha. Salvation is messy; like the flood, sometimes grace comes violently.

Still, there is God right in the middle of it—seeking, calling, inviting, reconciling, forgiving. He wants us to live (John

10:10), and calls us to life not just individually but communally. "For God so loved the *world*," we are told, that he sent his only Son (3:16).

The Ark of Your Local Parish

Did you know that the ark, not the cross, was the earliest symbol of Christ's Church on earth? It was not until the fourth century that the cross became the preeminent Christian symbol, following the victory of Emperor Constantine, who would later make Christianity legal with the Edict of Milan (AD 313). In the centuries preceding that historic decision, it was the ark that Christians looked to for salvation. The early Chur ch Fathers, the martyrs, and the saints all looked to the ark of the Church for hope. Consider the words of St. Cyprian of Carthage, who said, "If anyone could escape who was outside of the ark of Noah, then he also may escape who shall be outside of the Church."[5]

The ark is said to have rested atop Mount Ararat when the waters subsided (Genesis 8:4). I'd submit, however, that Noah's ark is nestled snuggly beside the parking lot of your local parish. Every Sunday the plank is thrown out to the world, ushering

> This Church of Christ, this ark, is a motley bunch.

aboard every type of animal, clean and unclean, inviting them to taste salvation and escape a world filled with hopelessness and, ultimately, death.

This Church of Christ, this ark, is a motley bunch. We're wannabe saints and willing sinners with one collective hope:

salvation. The poor pastor has the unenviable task of trying to get all of us into the ark and onto the same page as we set sail for eternity. The pastor's role is one of shepherd, there to direct, protect, and correct. Noah, the farmer and (now) sailor, definitely had some shepherd in him, as God entrusted him with leading his family into virtue when the rest of the world had chosen self.

Times change but truth does not. After so many centuries, God is still sending shepherds to gather our families and bring them to safety as storm clouds form on the horizon. God gave Noah a task when the skies were sunny. Onlookers no doubt thought him a fool. "Look at how good we have it!" his peers might have said. "Why rock (or build) the boat, Noah?"

The Problem with Not Rocking the Boat

Speaking of (not) rocking the boat, have you ever gathered together at a Thanksgiving meal where all the relatives tiptoed around the conversation, making sure that no arguments ensued? Because no one wants an uncomfortable holiday, we may just keep the conversation on a surface level, leaving things unsaid or staying away from controversial topics like religion or politics so as not to offend anyone.

That might be fine for one meal a year, when a host of extended family relatives are present, but if all your family meals were like that, something important would be missing. Close families often grow closer by confronting difficult issues and talking about it. Do we really demonstrate love when we fail to lovingly call one another out of sin or call one another on to greatness?

Ask yourself which family you prefer to live in? Family A, where real topics are glossed over and issues go unmentioned, or Family B, where it gets messy sometimes because people speak hard truths and challenge one another?

Would you rather be part of Family A, where success is measured more through shallow interaction or conflict avoidance? Family A will not challenge you, hold you accountable, or speak any truth to you that is too difficult for your "sensitive" psyche to handle. Family A is more concerned with looking good on the Christmas card than with interacting well the other days of the year.

Family B, on the other hand, cares more about your soul than your psyche. Fully aware of how pride begets laziness and how comfort can take precedence over true Christianity, Family B refuses to allow you to persist in sin or selfishness or to wallow in mediocrity. Out of love, Family B will drag you onto the mat to wrestle with demons, both internal and external.

By the way, Family A serves one perfect scoop of plain vanilla ice cream for dessert, in a perfect little bowl; Family B serves Rocky Road, straight out of the carton.

Often, the typical Catholic parish falls into one of these two categories. Parish A is all about comfort and not ruffling feathers. Transformation would be great, but at the end of the day, it's all about keeping the status quo so as to not upset too many people. It's the Thanksgiving meal where no one wants to offend, and so the gospel becomes inoffensive.

At Parish B, comfort food isn't on the menu. The priest cares more about your soul for eternity than for your mental "comfort" when preaching. He does not preach a vanilla homily because he knows that all roads *do not* lead to heaven. He exposes our infirmities but leads us to Christ and his mercy in the sacraments. He wants his people to become true disciples of Christ, and so he leads his people to pray and read the Scriptures. Parish B raises up evangelists to move outside the church walls and preach the good news to everyone they meet. Parish B calls her members out of the temptation to be lukewarm, "part-time Christians," as Pope Francis has said.

We need parishes that serve meat, not vanilla. A church bent on making people feel comfortable won't last because vanilla has no nutritional value. People want meat, and the only meat available was on Noah's cruise ship. There were three decks on Noah's mighty ark, but no comfort zone could be found.

The Church draws its power from love.

Of course, it's important to say here that none of this can exist without love; that is not the gospel. The Church draws its power from love. Without love, truth is mere doctrine. Without love, discipline will push away instead of drawing souls near. Without love, our preaching and works are in vain, as the great apostle St. Paul so importantly reminded us (1 Corinthians 13:1-3). Truth, yes, but truth that is spoken in love and offered through reconciliation.

And the responsibility to become Parish B lies not only with the pastor. All of us are called to discipleship, to show others what it looks like to be a true follower of Christ in real life.

That might require us to do a little boat rocking ourselves—always done, of course, with love, mercy, and compassion.

Do I Know Your Story?

Several years back, I plopped down on our sofa for our family movie night featuring the Disney classic *Bambi*. As the story progressed, I was struck not only by its simplicity and purity but also by the emotions it evoked in the hearts of my children. It didn't have the insanely high-tech effects of modern films. It didn't have sassy dialogue or the recognizable voices of stars. It was slow moving and gentle, yet somehow it held the attention of even my two-year-old. All of my girls' eyes were glued to the screen. And every one of them cuddled together tightly when (spoiler alert!) Bambi's mother died.

Not long after, I came across an article about Walt Disney, and one point in particular stood out to me. In November of 1938, following the commercial success of *Snow White*, the Disney brothers (Walt and Roy) bought their parents a mansion in North Hollywood. Several months later, however, an improperly installed furnace in the new home killed their mother, Flora, through carbon monoxide asphyxiation. The brothers were devastated and blamed themselves for the accident. It's said that the tragedy affected Walt at such a deep level that he never spoke about it, not even to his own children.

Just less than four years later, in August of 1942, the tale of Bambi, the little deer who lost his mother, hit the silver screen and became an instant classic. It is still touching young hearts with its timeless message about life, death, family, and friendship. I wonder if Walt Disney shared more than a story or just another animated movie in 1942. Perhaps he shared his cross. I don't know, of course, to what degree his own mother's death influenced *Bambi* or any of his future projects. What I do know is that everyone has a cross they bear. Some are more obvious than others. Some might seem heavier than others, but everybody is carrying one.

I've encountered many different kinds of people over my years serving in ministry, and I'm ashamed to say that I used to be quick to judge. I used to unintentionally "weigh" others' crosses against my own, believing that what I saw was all there was to them. The Holy Spirit has a funny way of broadening our perspective, if we let him. Too many times in my life, I was so busy lamenting the pain of my personal crosses that I refused to seek Christ's mercy or offer his mercy to others.

I started doing something a couple of years back that has really helped me grow in both my prayer life and in compassion. Whenever I encounter someone and we begin to converse—it could be a colleague, a waiter, or a disgruntled person in line— I say to myself, "Remember, their cross is twice as heavy as yours is." Since I began this little prayer exercise, my prayer for others has grown immeasurably and my criticisms of them have dissipated significantly. I decided to employ the same prayer before the start of Mass too, and it's made a significant difference in my experience of the liturgy.

Baptism Makes Us Family

Some Catholic parishes do hospitality really well. People know one another's names and stories. Other parishes seem to thrive on people wanting to be left alone. While the latter might be more popular to introverts and those in a hurry, it's not a full expression of the glory that is Catholicism. This isn't to say that everyone coming to Mass should feel as if it's a mixer or that the Mass should become merely a social engagement. Far from it.

It is to say, however, that we're all in this together, and that if Christ is to be taken at his word, we are not merely inhabitants of a diocese who happen to gather around an altar in the same zip code. No, we are a family; we are brothers and sisters by virtue of our baptism. The better I "know" you and know your story, the better I can pray with you and for you at Mass. In fact, that's the glory of the Mass and the genius of Catholicism: the Church is ushering all aboard the ark every Sunday, by Christ's command, and encouraging us to lift one another up. This is why getting to know our fellow parishioners ought to make us more eager to come to Mass and also

The Mass is also about God's people!

deepens our experience of it. That is why hospitality at Mass is so important and why engaging one another is so vital; it actually deepens our prayer.

The Mass is also a liturgy. A liturgy (from the Latin and Greek) is a "public work" done in the service of another. So the Mass isn't just about the priest and God or the priest and the meal; the Mass is also about God's people! I don't just show up with my kids and wife in tow because we are there to receive the Eucharist and hear the word, though both are indispensable to our lives and our sanity. No, I drag myself out of bed, get the kids ready, pile into the car, and navigate through traffic to get a space in the parking lot and in the pew . . . for the person next to me, and the person in front of me, and the person behind me.

At Mass we're there for the man who just lost his wife of fifty years and for the young couple preparing to be wed. We're there for the family struggling with their child's drug addiction and for the couple who is barren but desperately wants to conceive. We're there for the lonely single who is waiting for a future spouse, the serviceman's wife who prays nervously while he's deployed, the baptized Catholic who has wandered in after years away, and the visitor who is looking for "something more" and thinks that the Catholic Church just might have it. The pews represent every deck of the ark, housing every type of animal with one collective hope: salvation. Every person there is walking a walk, and I've been invited, not only to carry my own cross, but to act as their Simon of Cyrene, lightening the other person's load.

So Bambi and, by extension, Walt Disney remind me that things are not always how they appear to be on the surface. Everyone has a story, everyone carries a cross, and everyone needs a savior. In reality, that's the "magic kingdom"—it's the kingdom of heaven on earth, and it's being revealed to us at every single Mass.

Is your Sunday Mass experience a celebration? Does it celebrate a community of sinners seeking sainthood? Is the atmosphere hospitable or cold? Is it an environment where people feel welcomed or alienated, invited or judged? Are bodies and souls engaged or disengaged? Do people seek to know one another and walk with one another, or does this parish enter and exit merely as "Mass-goers" but not as "Church"? And before you say, "Well, that's not how the Church is in our (fill in the blank: diocese, state, region)," think again about those words from Pope Benedict XVI: "The world promises you comfort, but you were *not made for comfort*. You were made for greatness."

The Mass is about our tasting and experiencing the heavenly greatness for which we were created. The Mass, more than anything else in God's creation, calls us to true community and communion. We are supposed to be more than fellow Catholics who share little in common except a bond of our outward "religion." We are family, and the more invested the family of your parish is in one another, the more meaningful the celebration. When we bring ourselves—our hopes and dreams, fears and anxieties, successes and struggles—to the table with family and friends, the table is transformed into something far more meaningful. It's the table where hunger is satisfied—hunger for the Eucharist and for community.

This is where you hash it out. This is where you bring every struggle, every hurt, every wound, trusting that your heavenly Father, your Blessed Mother, and Christ your brother will understand your pain. This is the family dinner where you invite your brothers and sisters into your walk and enter into theirs.

And if they're hesitant, skittish, or standoffish at first, that's okay. Extend a hand. Offer a smile. A stranger is only a stranger until you introduce yourself. Be secure enough in yourself and in God's love for you that you allow others to see how God is at work in your life. You are a masterpiece of God, though unfinished. You are a work in progress, with the Potter's fingerprints all over you (Isaiah 64:8). What a gloriously messy reality to share. Mass isn't a place where we proclaim how perfect our family is. Mass is a place where we can stand imperfect but united, because our Father invites us to his Thanksgiving dinner table anyway.

Thanks be to God.

Questions for Reflection and Discussion

1. How often do your parish priest or other parishioners challenge you to be a more committed disciple of Jesus? How do you react to these challenges?

2. What does it mean to you to be a brother or sister in Christ to someone else? How is that relationship different from one based on common interests or work?

3. In what ways have you helped to carry the cross of another Christian, whether that person is a member of your parish, a neighbor, or a friend? How often have you let others know of your own crosses so that they can pray for you and support you?

4. How often do you introduce yourself to people you don't know at Mass? How can your parish grow in becoming more welcoming?

CHAPTER SEVEN

Wholly Holy: Understanding the Liturgy, Part I

*What graces, gifts, and virtues the
Holy Mass calls down.*
—St. Leonard of Port Maurice

A lot of parents bring their work home with them, figuratively speaking. My father, who always believed in doing things "big," did it—literally. My dad was a car man. After almost four decades in the car business, my father had done it all—credit, finance, sales, management, and ownership. Except for one thing: he had never personally rebuilt a car from the ground up. Apparently, he needed two things: time and free labor. One year my older brothers and I were drafted to help rebuild a 1965 Thunderbird, a magnificent gift to the automotive world. At least it was when we were finished.

Week after week, my father would arrive after a long day's work with more work to do. Some dads brought home pizza; mine brought home auto parts: bumpers, fenders, hubcaps, and door handles. Every part had to be perfect. We'd buff and shine. We'd polish and sandblast. Each son had a different job within the project, but each task, regardless of how small it seemed, mattered in the grand scheme of things.

Being the youngest at the time, my work focused more on the details than the power tools. That particular summer of my life, I used a toothbrush more on the car than on my teeth. It was exhausting work and oftentimes less than amusing. Still, we worked, often separately but somehow still "together." When we finished, we had accomplished more than a rebuild; we had made my father proud. The only thing that pleased him more than taking first place in our division of a classic car show was seeing his children working as one for a greater collective good.

Recently, it struck me during Mass how much that rebuild resembles the liturgy. When we come together, worship together, work and eat together, the Father is proud indeed. Nothing brings the family together like a project, and no project on earth brings the universal family together like the Mass does. Our family dinner table seats over one billion, and fortunately, we have the loaves-and fish-multiplier as our Lord, so we needn't worry about how many more join or return. God's kitchen is always open for business; his throne room has enough seating capacity for every soul on the planet and within the communion of saints (where there is no cry room with an obstructed view).

To fully appreciate the sacrifice and celebration of the Mass, however, we must know more than the destination; we must understand the journey there. The journey begins long before we ever pull into the parking lot of our church.

The Mass is the sum of many parts, seen and unseen. Liturgy doesn't just "happen." The Church offers us a cycle of readings. Musicians practice and prayerfully discern songs that will bring the Scriptures to life. Priests prayerfully prepare homilies. Lectors practice pronunciations of ancient names and faraway places.

No job preparing for good liturgy is irrelevant or unimportant. That being said, we must remember that we are merely Elijah atop the mountain. We prepare the altar for the sacrifice, we put the pieces in place, but it's God who does the heavy lifting. We set the table, but he prepares and becomes the meal.

We've spoken about the sacrifice of the Mass and the symbolism. We've covered the centrality of the priesthood and the community of worshippers that make up the Church universal, the Church of living stones built upon the cornerstone of

> We set the table, but God prepares and becomes the meal.

Christ. We've discussed the familial aspect of the liturgy and the importance of coming together as a family, united and fed at the table of the Lord.

When the rubber hits the road, however, or, more to the point, when our knees hit the kneelers, what exactly is transpiring? Yes, movements and symbols are outward earthly expressions of heavenly realities, as has been mentioned before, but what about the actual "parts" of the Mass? What does each of those mean? For if we are to appreciate the Mass as a whole, we must understand its parts.

Are You Prepared?

The Mass can be broken into two distinct liturgies: the Liturgy of the Word (which we will discuss in this chapter) and the Liturgy of the Eucharist (we'll save that for the next). While these are two distinctive parts, they are two sides of the same coin.

First come the Introductory Rites—the entrance antiphon, the greeting, the Penitential Act, and the "Collect" (prayer). Then begins the Liturgy of the Word, with its four readings; it ends after the Prayers of the Faithful. The Liturgy of the Eucharist begins with the presentation of gifts and ends after Communion but prior to the Concluding Rites.

Preparation for Mass actually begins days in advance. Our Church in her wisdom actually encourages and expects that we prayerfully read and contemplate the readings beforehand. With four readings, that might seem like a tall order. And yet think about it. Somehow we can usually find the time to read the news, check the sports score, watch the DVR recording of our favorite show, or comment on friends' Facebook walls. Why can't we carve out enough time to pray through the Mass readings ahead of time?

The truth is that many times we don't get more out of Mass because we don't bring much to it. Yet anytime in Scripture that the Father's children enter into the mystery more deeply, blessings come and grace flows. Contemplate the example of Mary of Bethany, whose desire to sit in the Lord's presence was praised above that of her sister, Martha, who scurried around performing tasks (Luke 10:38-42). Consider Zacchaeus, whose duplicity and dishonesty cheated earth but whose effort to see Jesus caught the eyes of heaven (19:1-20). Ponder Simon Peter, who, after lodging his doubt, "put out into the deep" anyway; his subsequent shock at the miraculous haul was outshone only by his increased self-awareness and growing humility (5:1-11). All three, whether still or active, entered into the Lord's mystery. The more proactive we are with God, the more responsive he is with us. The Lover does not force his love upon the beloved; he offers it and waits. He's invited us to the wedding banquet, yes, but there's still a hope-filled expectation that we'll come prepared (Matthew 22:1-14).

We can't "out-give" God. The more time we make to read and prepare, the more of the mystery there will be to behold: the sacred mystery that is the Mass will come more to life in our lives. Get to Confession if necessary! Contemplate what petitions you bring with you, what you need prayers for and guidance on, and place those prayers right at the foot of the altar. Take a page out of the magi's workbook: show up, bring your gifts, put them at his feet, and worship him. It's really that simple.

Now let's walk through the Mass step by step. Once we clearly see all the "pieces" and how (and when) they fit together, we start to grasp how the whole encounter in God's throne room takes shape. In understanding the "what" of the Mass, we'll more clearly see the "why" we do it. As my brothers and I did with my father's Thunderbird, let's break the Mass down into its parts, in hopes that what may seem antiquated to some might be made new again.

INTRODUCTORY RITES

Procession

Have you ever wondered why the priest, deacon, lectors, and servers process in? Wouldn't it be more efficient if they all just gathered in the sanctuary, and we started there?

Consider, however, what the procession signifies. Everyone is gathered in the church, and Christ (in the person of the priest) enters last, while we're all standing and singing God's praises. Indeed, Christ is present in each of us but uniquely so in the person of the priest, vested and prepared to offer a sacrifice on our behalf. Imagine a royal court with banner carriers, emissaries, and attendants all processing in before royalty, "preparing the way," as St. John the Baptist might say. As the priest joins the gathered family, our collective prayer and attention are drawn to the sanctuary, where all the action happens. In addition to the entrance hymn, there is often what is called an "entrance antiphon." Historically, every procession has always had a chant or song to accompany it. The entrance antiphon is a line from Scripture or tradition that is spoken or chanted to accompany the liturgical movement at that moment.

Bow

Notice the deep, reverent bow that takes place prior to entering the sanctuary. Throughout the liturgy, bowing and kneeling are outward expressions of our interior posture. More than a "nicety" or a mindless reactive ritual, the bow signifies that we are entering into a sacred space. The sanctuary mirrors the old Holy of Holies in Scripture, which only the high priest could enter—and only once a year—to offer sacrifice to God. Prior to Christ and his passion, a large veil separated the people from the inner sanctuary. Only certain people could enter into different parts of the Temple, and only the holiest could draw near. During Christ's crucifixion, the veil of the Temple was torn, and with it, through Jesus' blood, the separation between God and us was destroyed.

We are blessed to draw near (and if serving at Mass, even *into*) the sanctuary now, but the visible separation from the rest of the church (usually marked with steps and, historically, with a rail) offers us a visible reminder that this is far more than a "stage" for the priest but an offering place for the Lord. The depth of the bow and the reverence of the intermittent genuflections (if the tabernacle is in the sanctuary) are visible reminders of the hallowed ground upon which we tread.

Altar Kiss

Have you noticed that when the priest arrives and departs, he kisses the altar? This happens at his arrival even before the greeting or opening blessing. While Catholics know that Christ is truly present in his Body and Blood upon the altar later at Mass, far fewer ever learned that the altar itself is a symbol for Christ. When the priest or deacon kisses the altar, he is venerating Christ ("venerate" comes from a Latin word meaning to "adore" or to "revere").

Sign of the Cross

"In the name of the Father, and of the Son, and of the Holy Spirit." What do those words mean to you? For most of us cradle Catholics, we instinctively reach our right hand to our foreheads.

When we make the Sign of the Cross, however, we are marking ourselves with the greatest sign and act of love that the world has ever witnessed. Without the cross, we would have no hope of salvation. Without the cross, we would die. Without the cross of Jesus Christ, our past would dictate our future, which, to be clear, wouldn't be any future at all.

> ## Without the cross, we would die.

The Church doesn't begin each prayer with the Sign of the Cross because she lacks creativity; she begins with the sign of Christ's love because she wants to ensure that we never, ever forget its importance. In marking ourselves with the cross, we proclaim to the world and to ourselves who we are by demonstrating *whose* we are, thanking Christ for his ultimate sacrifice and example of love. We remind ourselves of the need to embrace suffering, abandon ourselves to the will of God, and pour out our own lives as a libation of love to all we encounter.

Benediction/Greeting

When the priest says, "The Lord be with you," we automatically reply, "And with your spirit." (Unless we have a 'brain freeze' and go back to the old way of responding, "And also with you.") This opening admonition from the priest, however, is far from a nice "churchy" way of saying, "Good morning" or "Howdy." This greeting is reserved for epic moments in salvation history, times in Scripture in which God is warning and reminding those he loves that there is a dangerous mission before them (which we'll discuss in greater detail later). Simply put, this greeting is both a reminder that God is with us, personally and communally (Matthew 18:20), and a plea for his divine grace and strength to remain with us, because we're going to need it for what we are about to experience.

So why is it so important to say, "and with your *spirit*"? First, because this response is more than an informal "What's up?" greeting to a priest you happen to know. This is a formal greeting from the priest (or deacon), to which the people respond. Throughout the history of the Church, such a response has been directed to the very core of who that person is. When St. Paul wrote to St. Timothy, he addressed his spirit (2 Timothy 4:22), and in the early Church (around AD 215), St. Hippolytus wrote about how the people responded to the priests by offering greetings to their very spirits. The importance of the priest, who stands in the person of Christ as the leader of the people, is emphasized in this more formal and faithful response. As you say it, pray for the priest, that he might continue to live his priesthood with faith and enthusiasm for his people. And consider it like a return blessing when you give his greeting right back to him—but to his *spirit*, the core of who he is as a priest.

You'll notice this same greeting and response a few times during Mass. Try to pay attention to when and where it takes place within the liturgy, as it's usually a signal that something very challenging is about to happen.

Penitential Act

As we come into Mass, we are often burdened with things that we have done throughout the week—either sins against God or against one another—that can cause tension or distance between God and us. At the beginning of the Mass, we always first acknowledge the fact that we need to set things right in order to be able to offer the highest form of prayer we know as Catholics. At the Penitential Act, we do more than just "clear the air." We humbly announce our fault and our need for forgiveness of any sins that we might have committed. To be "penitential" means to be sincerely sorry for something, and a "rite" is a solemn ceremony or action.

Oftentimes we pray what's called the *Confiteor*, which begins, "I confess to almighty God and to you, my brothers and sisters . . . " In it we confess that we are sinners and say, "I have greatly sinned . . . through my fault, through my fault, through my most grievous fault." Each time we repeat that phrase, we should go deeper and deeper into our hearts, calling to mind all those things we have done that have lacked charity, offended God, or hurt our neighbor. And not only does the Church ask us to admit our *most grievous fault*, but she also asks us to physically show our need for repentance by striking our chests three times as we say the words. This associates a physical action with our words in order to give our worship a fuller meaning. We're not literally beating ourselves up about it, but showing ourselves—and one another—that as we sin in a bodily way, we repent in a bodily way too.

The Church is inviting us to realize that if we're going to say we're sorry, we need to really mean it. We need to do more than just gloss over it. This prayer is not just about saying that we're sorry and asking for forgiveness; we are also admitting that it is *our fault,* and we need God's forgiveness and the prayers of our community to avoid sin again.

One important thing to remember: although we acknowledge our need for forgiveness, notice that the priest does not give absolution at the end of this rite. Rather, the priest asks that God will have mercy on us. We know that the Eucharist will forgive any venial sins, but we need to go to the Sacrament of Reconciliation to be forgiven of serious and habitual sin.

Kyrie (Lord, Have Mercy)

Sometimes it feels like a short liturgical "tennis match" back and forth with the priest or deacon. He says a prayer, and we respond, "Lord, have mercy," and then, "Christ, have mercy," and then once again, "Lord, have mercy." Again, it can be dangerously automatic. Do you desire the divine mercy of God? I know I do. I am a sinner striving for sainthood but falling painfully short most days. Do you *need* Christ's mercy? You better believe you do. We all do. Do we *yearn* for our Lord's mercy? We ought to, even more than a baby yearns for milk or a Chicago Cubs fan yearns for a World Series championship. Yes, we need God's mercy more than the air we breathe. The Church in her wisdom not only recognizes our need; she pauses and encourages us to collectively pray for God's mercy before we go any further into the sacrifice of the Mass. Like a good mother, the Church is always one step ahead of us.

Some parishes use the Greek for this prayer and sing it in chant: "*Kyrie eleison*" and "*Christe eleison.*" Even when the rest of the Mass was in Latin, this was the only prayer that remained in Greek. Remember, the early Church spoke Greek, even in Rome.

Gloria/Collect

Okay, name the moment in the Bible when we hear these words sung: "Glory to God in the highest, and on earth peace to people of good will." If you haven't remembered the line yet, here's a hint: it was sung one silent, holy night (cf. Luke 2:14). It was the voices of angels, erupting in praise of God's incarnate presence in this world. A few miles outside of Jerusalem, in the rolling hills surrounding Bethlehem, shepherds were the first to enjoy the chorus, and two thousand years later we still sing or say it at Mass (except during Advent and Lent).

This is fitting, since the Mass is not only a celebration of Christ's sacrifice but, in a way, of Christmas. At every Mass we celebrate Jesus' enduring presence among us and within us. St. Matthew reminds us at the beginning of his Gospel that Jesus is Emmanuel, which means, "God with us" (1:23); he concludes his work echoing this truth, reminding us of Christ's promise to be with us always, "to the close of the age" (28:20). The promise of God's presence with and for us "bookends" Matthew's Gospel and is experienced at every single Catholic Mass. The angels, too, worship beside us during Mass, erupting in songs and hymns that our earthly ears can't hear but that someday our heavenly voices will join in singing. So if you have a difficult time getting your kids to Church, let them know it's Christmas every Sunday, and that after we sing, God is bringing us *presence* far better than Santa's.

When the priest says, "Let us pray," it is actually an invitation to the people to offer a prayer in their hearts to God to prepare for Mass. The collect "collects" those silent prayers of the people and offers them all to God in one universal prayer of the Church.

LITURGY OF THE WORD

The first Scripture verse we hear our Lord quote in the Gospels comes from the Book of Deuteronomy (8:3). While being tempted by Satan, Jesus says, "Man shall not live by bread alone / but by every word that proceeds from the mouth of God" (Matthew 4:4; cf. Luke 4:4).

Now consider this truth in light of the Mass: we don't just show up and receive the Eucharist. At Mass we first *hear* the word of God during the readings and psalm response. It is in Sacred Scripture that our Father feeds us with his timeless truth. Only then are we nourished by the Word of God, who is Jesus Christ, the timeless Word that came forth from God. If we have, indeed, been reading and praying with the Mass readings ahead of time and ruminating, yes, chewing on them like the prophet Jeremiah (15:16), then by the time the lector gets up to the ambo to proclaim them, we'll be ready. Our hearts will be open; our spiritual eyes, focused; and our hearing, sharpened. That word "proclaim" is important. Notice that we aren't instructed to just sit and read these passages on our own in the pews. Rather, the word of God is publicly and forcefully proclaimed for all to hear as one body, binding us to its truth and to one another. That proclamation of God's truth demands an active response.

First Reading

The first reading normally comes to us from the Old Testament, with the notable exception of the Easter season, when it comes exclusively from St. Luke's Acts of the Apostles. Given that most of us don't have a strong command of Biblical allegory, Mediterranean culture, or the history of Israel, it's often useful to have a good Catholic Study Bible with solid footnotes available to help us unpack the fullness of the readings proclaimed. Oftentimes you'll notice a strong thematic parallel between the first reading and the Gospel. Pay attention to it. The Church in her wisdom not only gives us a three-year cycle of readings, but prayerfully arranges them to offer consistent and obvious themes

> The more we understand the stories of our ancestors in faith, the better we'll come to understand our own.

that eclipse time and span the centuries. While idiomatic expressions evolve and cultures change, you'll notice that the truth of God is timeless. The more we understand the stories of our ancestors in faith, the better we'll come to understand our own.

Psalm Response

The psalm response is often sung because the psalms are just that—songs. The psalms play an important part in the Church's liturgy. Even though weekday Masses don't usually have a second reading, they always have a psalm response, and the Liturgy of the Hours, or Divine Office, the universal prayer of the Church, is rooted in the psalms.

A closer examination of the Book of Psalms reveals something intriguing: roughly two-thirds of the 150 psalms are psalms of lament (from the Latin for "weeping"). The psalms aren't just happy-go-lucky songs that proclaim God's greatness, although some are. They speak to the reality of our existence and collective struggle. Our lives are roller coasters. One minute we feel connected to God, the next we strain to feel his presence in our lives. One day we trust in his love, the next we feel abandoned. These are common themes recorded three thousand years ago in the psalms but still true in our lives today.

Flip through the psalms and pray these songs on your own. Many have been recorded by some of the biggest names in music because they capture the longings and struggles of the heart so perfectly. The psalms are a great reminder that "when we sing, we pray twice," as St. Augustine is often quoted as saying.

Second Reading

The second reading comes from the New Testament letters and epistles, often from the pen of St. Paul. For me, it functions as a biblical "Where's Waldo?" because I have to figure out (if I haven't read the readings ahead of time) who the letter is directed to. Corinth? Ephesus? Perhaps the good people of Thessalonica?

It is usually not as easy to discern why the second reading is included with the first reading and Gospel, so don't get dismayed if you can't figure out the tie-in at first. One clue: it often provides a practical example of what is required when the other readings are lived out.

St. Paul, St. Peter, and the other New Testament writers were not trying to give us another Gospel—far from it. Instead, they were trying to explain to the early Church—and to us— what living as a Christian was supposed to look like. This was a new way of life. People in the various church communities were still trying to figure out what to hold onto from the Jewish law and what to let go of. St. Paul's Letter to the Galatians, for instance, is an ongoing treatise on whether newly baptized Christians still needed to be circumcised. Miss that point, and you miss the point of the letter. So the more we know of each epistle, the more each letter will come to life for us on a practical level. Take time to read the introductions to each of the New Testament letters, and you'll be amazed at how much the Liturgy of the Word fires your neurons each Sunday.

Gospel Proclamation

The *Catechism of the Catholic Church* proclaims that the Gospels are "the heart of all the Scriptures" (125) and that they hold "a unique place in the Church" (127), which explains why we stand for the reading of the Gospel. In the wheel of the Church, the Gospels are the axles; they are both the door and the hinge to everything we believe. They are the foundation for all the Church teaches and holds dear. While the whole of Sacred Scripture is to be venerated, the Gospels are placed on an even higher level of veneration. These are not merely words about God; the Gospels record the words of God himself, incarnate and on a mission.

The Gospels ought to promote a sense of urgency in our lives, and so when we hear them at Mass, our posture is that of standing instead of sitting. We, like Mary, ought to be so inspired ("inspire" means to "breathe in") by God's message of love that we, too, need to make "haste" to share it, as Mary did (Luke 1:39). The Gospels not only record for us how God responded to his people, but also how God moves and thinks and loves. Ripe for deeper reflection, the Gospels bid us into the very heart of God.

Lean into them when you read them or when you hear them proclaimed by the priest or deacon. Enter into the story in a manner reminiscent of *lectio divina* (Latin for "sacred reading"). When Jesus enters the Jordan to be baptized, go with him. When Jairus comes to the Master seeking healing for his terminally ill daughter, see the compassion on Jesus' brow (Luke 8:41-42). When Jesus arrives to find that Lazarus has died, watch the tears fall from our Savior's face (John 11:35). The Gospels don't just tell us about how God interacted with the people in the stories, but how God, today, interacts with us. There may be no more poignant moment in your week than standing beside your loved ones and hearing how much God loves us and how actively he seeks our salvation, then and now.

Homily

As mentioned previously, the priesthood of too many men is judged on nothing more than homilies. There is not much more to be said than was covered in chapter 5, except this: never underestimate the courage it takes to proclaim truth to a culture that does not desire it. It's easy for a priest to pitch a softball to his people, waxing poetic about his last vacation or a memory from his childhood. These stories are interesting and they personify the priest in many ways, making the seemingly inaccessible and enigmatic priesthood somehow "accessible" to those of us not living in rectories and embracing celibacy. That being said, consider the risk and beauty of the priest who goes out on a limb speaking truth about the areas of our lives that we don't want to hear about—social justice, finances, sexuality, addiction, self-ishness, politics, or difficult moral questions. These courageous souls deserve our praise, not our condemnation.

During the homily, the priest (or deacon) offers insight into how we are to live out the truths that have just been proclaimed. The old adage of "Don't kill the messenger" might need to be employed on certain Sundays. Before we judge too harshly or heap praise too freely, remember that the priest is charged by his bishop and, more important, by God to pastor his flock toward heaven. The road to heaven is narrow, but the road to hell has an HOV lane. Encourage your priest to challenge his flock with the truth while showing mercy to the sinner, just as Christ did and charged us *all* to do (Luke 17:3).

> You are the faithful, and your prayers are needed desperately.

Prayers of the Faithful

The "faithful" includes you—you are the faithful, and your prayers are needed desperately by those in power, those in peril, and those not able to be in the pews on any given Sunday. In offering these prayers, we fulfill St. Paul's directive to St. Timothy:

> First of all, then, I urge that supplications, prayers, intercessions, and thanksgivings be made for all men, for kings and all who are in high positions, that we may lead a quiet and peaceable life, godly and respectful in every way. This is good, and it is acceptable in the sight of God our Savior, who desires all men to be saved

and to come to the knowledge of the truth. For there is one God, and there is one mediator between God and men, the man Christ Jesus. (1 Timothy 2:1-5)

You might spot a "formula" within the Prayers of the Faithful. The first prayers normally focus on newsworthy events such as natural disasters, acts of violence, war, and so forth. We speak to and invite God into the realities of our suffering and sin. Next, we turn to world events, such as praying for world leaders and for a greater respect for the poor and for human life and dignity. The formula often moves from the global to the local—from prayers for the world to prayers for our country and the armed forces. Prayers are sometimes offered for justice issues in our country, like an end to abortion or the fight for religious freedom. Prayers continue for the parish, its ministries and ministers, and its initiatives. Finally, prayers are offered for the sick and the dead from our parish family, reminding us that we are all interconnected and that our home is not here.

By the way, as the passage from 1 Timothy 2:5 affirms, Christ is the "one mediator between God and men." We invite others into our lives to pray with and for us, and we invite the saints to pray with and for us, as they are also alive (even more alive than we are!). Intercessory prayer, prayer for one another, is a secondary mediation; we are inviting our brothers and sisters, both here on earth and fully alive in heaven, to join their prayers to ours as we collectively put them at the feet of Jesus. In this moment of the Mass, we are joining our prayers to the communion of saints *and to the Church universal*, over one billion strong. That's a lot of grace!

Questions for Reflection and Discussion

1. What are the steps you take prior to Sunday morning to prepare yourself for Mass? If your answer is none, what might you commit to doing in the future?

2. How would you explain to another Catholic why reading and praying with the Sunday readings ahead of time is so important?

3. What movement/action within the Mass do you most often do "reactively" without thinking (i.e., the Sign of the Cross, blessing yourself with holy water)? How can you do this more intentionally? What do you think would be the result?

4. What point or explanation struck you as the most intriguing or the most often forgotten element within the first half of the Mass?

CHAPTER EIGHT

Wholly Holy:
Understanding the Liturgy,
Part II

*Every consecrated host is made to burn itself up
with love in a human heart.*
—St. John Vianney

You want a Bible study? At Mass the Scriptures come to life like no other place on earth. The liturgy is Scripture in 3D, as the once-and-for-all, timeless sacrifice of Calvary is made "present" again in the sanctuary, just as you read about in the Gospels. You're not just worshipping in imitation of the angels; you're worshipping *alongside them,* just as you read about in the Book of Revelation. We're not trying to "recreate" God's throne room within our church building; God is lifting us up into his heavenly throne room for an hour. The Mass is less about God "coming down" as it is about God *lifting us up.* The Eucharist and indeed the Mass are a foretaste of heaven—especially as we begin the Liturgy of the Eucharist, getting closer to the climactic moment when we will receive Jesus in Holy Communion.

Presentation of Gifts (Offertory)
The Liturgy of the Eucharist begins with the presentation of the gifts and the preparation of the altar. Notice that while our

donations are being offered and brought forward, so are the gifts. This is more than our making sure that the parish bills are paid; this is deciding whether, like Cain and Abel, we will give our "first fruits" to God. In Genesis, Abraham gives one-tenth of his property as a sacrificial offering to God (28:22), which is where the word "tithe," meaning "10 percent," comes from. In the Gospel, Jesus heals ten lepers, but only one returns to give thanks (Luke 17:11-19). The newly cleansed become the 10 percent, a living

> We offer back to God all our gifts and talents, and our very lives.

embodiment of a tithe. While the Church does not require a literal giving of 10 percent of our income, we should be giving our first fruits—not withholding from God, but offering them up in a spirit of love and gratitude.

We offer our alms and the elements of bread and wine, yes, but we are also supposed to be offering our prayers and ourselves. Truthfully, this is when we place ourselves on the altar of sacrifice. We offer back to God all our gifts and talents and our very lives—which are all from him anyway—for his glory (Romans 12:1-2). In essence, we are effectively walking into the sanctuary and lying down upon the altar, offering our lives in honor of our Father, much like Isaac did (Genesis 22). Only after we've given ourselves to the Father can we truly "lift up our hearts" when the priest invites us to do so moments later.

As we move further into the Liturgy of the Eucharist, we'd all be well served to have a close-up view. There are several seemingly subtle movements on the part of the priest that are noteworthy but easily missed. I'd like to mention a few here.

Have you ever noticed the priest or deacon diluting the wine with water? You may be thinking, "Makes sense. That wine is really sweet." Well, yes, but it's so much more than that. Remember, within the Mass, *every movement has a purpose*; every movement communicates a deeper truth.

When the water and wine are mingled, it's supposed to point us toward the Incarnation. Water symbolizes the earthly; wine, the divine. When we see the water and wine commingle, we are supposed to be reminded of how God took human flesh. We are also supposed to rejoice in the fact that we humans have been invited to become partakers of God's divine nature (2 Peter 1:4). What became wine by Christ's hand in Cana? Water. What poured out of Christ's side, giving birth to the Church atop Calvary on Good Friday? Blood and water flowed (John 19:34). More than a simple gesture of dilution, this action has theological symbolism and significance.

Another subtle movement is when the priest turns and washes his hands. More than a salute to us "germaphobes," this action is symbolic of the priest recognizing his own sinfulness. The basin or bowl used to wash the priest's hands is called the *lavabo* (Latin for "I will wash"). During this moment of ceremonial washing, the priest actually quotes from the prayer of King David in Psalm 51:2: "Lord, wash away my iniquity and cleanse me from my sin." In that moment of ceremonial cleansing, the priest is beseeching the Lord, and we are reminded that although the priest, too, can be sinful, God is bigger than our sin and more merciful than we can ever comprehend.

THE EUCHARISTIC PRAYER

Preface

The Preface is when we hear the familiar liturgical trifecta:

> The Lord be with you.
> *And with your spirit.*
> Lift up your hearts.
> *We lift them up to the Lord.*
> Let us give thanks to the Lord our God.
> *It is right and just.*

You've heard it. You've responded. How often, though, do you think about what you're saying? One of the dangers of our prayers at Mass is that they can become reactive rather than proactive. A priest of God is praying that God's spirit will be very much alive and animated within you. Why? Because you're going to need the power of the Holy Spirit to acquiesce to what you're about to do.

What are you about to do?

Lay your life, hopes, dreams, fears, anxieties—your very self—upon the altar, to be consumed and transformed by the God of the universe, that's all.

Go ahead and read that sentence again. It's dense.

We can't be dense, however, to the magnitude of what we're praying at this moment of the liturgy. We are not just responding; we are giving God permission to take, break, and remake our lives in him. Think hard about this moment and whether or not you mean what you say—and pray. At this moment of the Mass, we give God our everything, echoing how he gave his everything to us.

Sanctus

Whether uttered or sung, "Hosanna" is proclaimed in what many refer to as the "Holy, Holy, Holy" prayer.

Holy, Holy, Holy Lord God of hosts.
Heaven and earth are full of your glory.
Hosanna in the highest.
Blessed is he who comes in the name of the Lord.
Hosanna in the highest.

Now with the new translation, some parishes are adding in a little more Latin here and there. In addition, some music ministries are utilizing some of the Latin words in more modern arrangements. So you might hear these words or lyrics, which are the exact Latin translation of the prayer above:

Sanctus, Sanctus, Sanctus Dominus Deus Sabbaoth.
Pleni sunt caeli et terra gloria tua.
Hosanna in excelsis.
Benedictus qui venit in nomine Domini.
Hosanna in excelsis.

The exclamation of "Holy, Holy, Holy" is found in Scripture in both Isaiah 6:1-5 and Revelation 4:2-8. Both passages unveil images of God's heavenly throne room and the ceaseless worship that is eternally happening there.

When we sing the *Sanctus*, we are joining in the song of the angels in heaven. It is pure worship, a humble reaction to the majesty of God. It's a song of praise celebrating God's presence. Proclaiming it within the Mass at that moment is, likewise, a celebration of God's presence among us. Just as in the passages from Isaiah and Revelation (which you should read on your own), we ought to be filled with an earth-shattering, soul-stirring *awe* that God would make his presence known to us in this way.

Try learning the Latin version of the *Sanctus* if you don't already know it. It's a way of broadening your prayer life, and it enables you to pray with Catholics of other cultures in a common language.

Epiclesis

Mentioned earlier, the *epiclesis* is a monumental moment within the liturgy. From the Greek, meaning "to call down," it's an invocation of the Holy Spirit, signified by the sweeping-down motion of the priest's hands over the gifts upon the altar. Note: it's not the priest but the priest's prayer that changes the gifts upon the altar. The *epiclesis*, directed to God the Father through the Holy Spirit, is a prayer for the gifts to be transformed and for that transformation to bring about a reception of grace on the part of all of us gathered. This is the Holy Trinity at work par excellence: the Father shows his love manifested through Christ the Son and sanctified by the love of the Holy Spirit. How's that for a theologically deep and oversimplified sentence? Just as the priests of the Old Testament (and old covenant) raised their hands atop the sacrifice, the hands of Christ through his priests now sanctify ordinary elements to elevate them to the level of divine.

You want to behold a mystery? Look no further than your local altar as the priest invokes the power of the almighty One.

Consecration

One can normally tell when the consecration is happening in my parish, not because the priest is holding up the host or the chalice, but because that's usually when my youngest child decides to erupt in discontent.

During the consecration (Latin for "dedicated as sacred"), the lowly bread and wine become nothing less than the highest of all creation, the very Body and Blood of our Lord and Savior, Jesus Christ.

Stop and consider the magnitude of truth in that last sentence. *God* is made present upon the altar . . . for you and for me. God fulfills his promise never to leave us (Matthew 28:20). We are actually able to take part in—to "partake" in—God's divine nature (2 Peter 1:4). This reality deserves contemplation.

The priest elevates both the bread and the wine, and that subtle liturgical movement and moment deserve mention. The elevation ought to draw our minds back to the "elevations" in Scripture—of Moses with the healing saraph serpent in the desert (Numbers 21:4-9) and of Christ elevated upon the cross to redeem our sins. Alluding to his death on the cross, Jesus himself recounts the story of the serpent during his twilight discussion with Nicodemus (John 3:14-15).

During the 1200s, St. Eudes de Sully, a bishop in France, began elevating the gifts in a pronounced way. If you look closely, you'll notice five elevations during Mass, both minor (subtle) and major (noticeable), to signify something important happening. The elevations make present the past and beckon us toward the future throughout the timeless liturgy.

Memorial Acclamation

Three acclamations can now be used at Mass from the new translation of the Roman Missal. Here is one of them:

> We proclaim your Death, O Lord,
> and profess your Resurrection
> until you come again.

None of us doubt that Christ died. Almost none of us doubt that Christ rose. Judging by decisions many of us make on a weekly basis, however, one could make the argument that a large percentage of us doubt or possibly forget that Christ is coming back. The good news is that he's already here, at this exact moment, upon the altar in his glorified flesh and blood. The even better news is that he gives us this flesh and blood to fill us with his life (grace) that we might be ready when he does come back again. It's not enough to say it, however; we need to think about it. Notice, too, that once we've prayed it, we kneel. So powerful is this proclamation and reality that we are reduced to silence, and our posture is guided to even deeper reverence.

The Anamnesis

Anamnesis is Greek for "memorial," and it's used because we are "remembering" Christ's self-sacrifice and death upon the cross in these moments. Remember (no pun intended) that while Christ is not being "re-crucified" in any way, in God's timelessness we are being transported back in time to Calvary. In this moment, we get to participate as a Church in what Jesus did on the cross; our tiny sacrifices are being taken up and joined with his perfect sacrifice. Our prayers, pains, struggles, doubts, joys, blessings, hopes, and dreams are all being elevated and perfected as we offer them (through the priest, who is Christ) to our Father in heaven. We see now, once again, why it is so important that we *bring* something to the Mass—some intention—along with us.

> Our prayers, pains, struggles, doubts, joys, blessings, hopes, and dreams are all being elevated and perfected.

Depending upon which Eucharistic Prayer is used (there are four of them), the priest prays, "Look, we pray, upon the oblation [offering or sacrifice] of your Church" or "Be pleased to look upon these offerings with a serene and kindly countenance." Listen closely to the words within these prayers as they reiterate these truths. They contain profound and powerful realities. The more attention we pay to them, the better we will pray.

The Doxology

From the Greek for "a word of praise," a *doxology* is usually defined as a "short hymn of praise to God." I believe, however, that such a definition fails to do it justice or to capture the essence of the praise it signifies. I like to describe it to my children as an *eruption* of praise to God. The doxology during the Eucharistic

Prayer builds in momentum and power. Every Eucharistic Prayer ends with a great doxology, as the priest elevates the sacred Body and Blood of Jesus and exclaims:

> Through him, and with him, and in him,
> Oh God, almighty Father,
> in the unity of the Holy Spirit,
> all glory and honor is yours,
> for ever and ever. Amen.

The "him" in question is Jesus, of course, who is being elevated in glory in the same way that he was elevated upon the cross and at his ascension. All eyes, hearts, and souls are called into the liturgical movement of the elevation, capturing our attention on what, just minutes ago, was simple bread and wine yet now is inconceivably more. This is our Savior. This is the Lamb sent to take our sins away. This is the One who came to redeem us. This is the God of the universe, the Holy Trinity in its totality, offering us the Body and Blood of Christ!

The only acceptable response is one of praise, not merely spoken but sung, as we collectively affirm in one voice . . .

The Great Amen

More than a song, the Great Amen is an expression and affirmation of our belief *in* and love *for* Jesus Christ who is now present in our midst, the God who comes to save us from the inside out. That's why we proclaim, not a personal amen or a private, silent amen, but a corporate and *great* amen loud enough that the angels ought to cover their ears with their wings (if they had wings or ears).

THE COMMUNION RITE

The following moments are quite special and uniquely sacred. The Lord is present upon the altar, and each liturgical movement that follows must take this reality into consideration. The highest reverence is expected and appropriate. Note, too, that these actions happen only *after* God is present upon the altar.

The Lord's Prayer

Consider the timing. We could have prayed this most famous prayer (from Matthew 6 and Luke 11) at any moment within the Mass, but we have waited until the Lord has been made present upon the altar. This prayer, given to us by the "perfect pray-er," Christ himself, is directed to his Father and our Father. An entire book could be written about the beauty, depth, and danger of this prayer. (In fact, I have written one entitled *The "R" Father* that expresses far more fully this gift from God.) Let us never forget what a beautiful gift we have in the simplicity and sublimity of this prayer.

The Rite of Peace

We're all aware of that moment during Mass when it's time for the sign of peace. For some folks, the moment is uncomfortable, made obvious by their desire not to touch or interact with any of their brothers or sisters in Christ sitting near them. For others, it is an entirely different story; the hugs and handshakes can go on indefinitely if the music ministry does not quickly move the assembly into the Lamb of God.

The history and evolution of the sign of peace, or, as it used to be known, the kiss of peace, is quite interesting; for such a simple action, the development is surprisingly extensive. We pick up our story in the time of St. Justin Martyr (early fourth century), who recorded and taught that the people exchanged the kiss of peace during the Prayer of the Faithful, greeting each other with a kiss. By the fourth century, the Church in Rome and throughout most of the Italian peninsula began to offer a kiss of peace only before Communion.

St. Paul's letters usually begin and end with such wishes for a communion of peace among all the members of a particular church. The gesture of extending the hands during the offering of peace was originally a kind of collective embrace. For centuries, it remained a private prayer for the priest. Nowadays, the manner of giving the sign of peace is to be determined locally and should take into account the character and customs of the people. In the United States, the embrace or the kiss on the cheek was never widespread custom, but the handshake has served a similar function.

The sign of peace is not a "break" from Mass or a moment for us to forget what and, more to the point, who is present in the sanctuary. Each of us is invited at this time to genuinely make peace—with our spouse, our kids, or our neighbors, both figuratively and literally—for any and all wrongs we have perpetrated against them. This is less a moment for "high fives" and more a moment for bowing low, as we have failed our loved ones but are seeking God's grace to do better going forward.

Lamb of God (Agnus Dei)

We talked about the meaning of the title "Lamb of God" in chapter 5. Here we repeat the words of St. John the Baptist, who proclaimed Jesus as "the Lamb of God, who takes away the sin of the world" (John 1:29). We are begging Jesus, the Lamb of God, to have mercy on us for our sins. We are asking him to give us his grace and peace of mind, heart, and soul.

Consider these words from Psalm 71:23: "My lips will shout for joy, / when I sing praises to thee; / my soul also, which thou hast rescued." This verse really convicts me. It's a great reminder to us all that our worship is supposed to be a passionate, Spirit-filled response to the greatness and love of God the Father. Whether we are singing or responding during Mass, it

> Singing is not merely a physical act but also a spiritual one.

should never be just a boring, half-audible response but rather a *shout* from the depths of our souls, one filled with joy. (Obviously, this shout doesn't need to be loud in volume.) This verse also tells us that singing invites, involves, and ignites our souls; that at Mass, as in all worship, singing is not merely a physical act but also a spiritual one.

Some parishes sing the Lamb of God in Latin. Latin is sometimes referred to as a "dead" language. But this language isn't dead because if we are really praying it, it brings life. Here is the Lamb of God in Latin:

Agnus Dei, qui tollis peccata mundi,
Miserere nobis
Agnus Dei, qui tollis peccata mundi,
Miserere nobis

Agnus Dei, qui tollis peccata mundi,
Dona nobis pacem.

Fraction Rite

The fraction rite actually begins while the congregation is singing or reciting the Lamb of God. It's another subtle yet pronounced moment within the Liturgy of the Eucharist. The priest takes a piece of the now consecrated bread, breaks it off, and drops it into the chalice of wine transubstantiated into Christ's sacred Blood.

Just as Christ broke the loaves of bread during his miraculous feeding of the five thousand, during the Last Supper, and for the travelers once they reached Emmaus (Luke 9:16-17; 22:1-22; 24:13-35), the priest now breaks the bread once again. Note, though, that the Body is not just broken but commingled with the Blood.

In ancient Judaism, when the priest would sacrifice the lamb, he would drain its blood. Only once the blood was distinct and fully separated from the animal was the animal considered dead. Imagine, now, what would happen if a priest of the old covenant before Christ was transported to a modern-day Mass. The body and blood of this sacrifice is not separated, signaling death, but united, *signaling life.* During the fraction rite, we see the fullness of life that Christ Jesus promised us all (John 10:10).

Communion

At this moment during Mass, we proclaim a prayer that comes right out of the Gospel:

Lord, I am not worthy
that you should enter under my roof,
but only say the word
and my soul will be healed.

Take a minute to read through the scene in your Bible where Jesus is approached by a centurion whose servant is paralyzed (Matthew 8:5-13). Now remember, Jews and Gentiles did not like one another very much. They were forbidden to interact with one another, which is one of the reasons why Jesus was constantly getting into so much trouble with the Jewish religious leaders of that time.

The idea of a Jewish teacher going to the home of a gentile officer (centurion) would have been shocking and scandalizing to any Jew. A centurion exercises great authority over an army of powerful people, which is yet another reason that his own proclamation of Jesus' authority is so impressive (Matthew 8:9). Here he is, publicly affirming Jesus' identity and humbly begging him to heal his servant. Additionally, he proclaims his own unworthiness for Christ to enter his dwelling place.

So too do we now acknowledge our own unworthiness for Christ to enter under the "roof" of our souls in Holy Communion. Yet just as the centurion believed that Christ could heal his servant, we, as Christ's servants, also believe that he can and will heal us of our unworthiness before our Eucharistic encounter.

St. Paul reminds us that our bodies are temples (1 Corinthians 6:19). When we receive Jesus Christ in the Holy Eucharist, he is literally coming under the roof of our temples. As he enters under our roof, he transforms us into living, walking tabernacles that are sent out into the world. As the *Catechism of the Catholic Church* reminds us, "Before so great a sacrament, the faithful can only echo humbly and with ardent faith the words of the Centurion" (1386).

It might initially feel strange to pray "under my roof" when speaking about our own bodily temples, but it's an opportunity to pray in a more contemplative way. Place yourself within the scene in this passage. Feel the humidity in the air and the dirt beneath your feet. Listen to the humble boldness echoing out of the centurion's words and the joyful response such humility evokes in the heart of Jesus. Hold on to that image when you pray these words, and pray them with all of your heart.

It's at this moment that we receive and consume the Body and Blood of Christ, the God of the universe. That is the quin-tessential reality of your Catholicism, and worthy of deep contemplation.

Communion Meditation

So deep is this reality of our consuming and being consumed by the love of Jesus Christ that we need to pause silently and contemplate it. To "contemplate" means, in Latin, to "observe." More to the point, this part of the Mass is called the *meditation*, which means to "measure." What are we contemplating and measuring, one might wonder? How God could be so humble as to dwell within us (Philippians 2:6-7; Colossians 3:16; 2 Peter 1:4).

As St. Alphonsus Liguori reminded us, there is no moment within the course of our week that we are more closely united to the sacred heart of Jesus and to our loved ones who have gone before us to heaven than in the moments immediately following our reception of the Eucharist at Mass. While we kneel down, together as one body but singularly grateful, we are like the apostles, in awe of the singular gift of life that the Lord has granted us in the wake of life's storms (Matthew 14:33).

CONCLUDING RITE

Final Blessing

Every good action movie has that one moment when all eyes are on the hero as he readies himself (or herself) to face some high-risk, against-all-the-odds mission. Maybe there is a toast, a bow, a cheer, a song—something ceremonial that signifies that the hero is accepting his destiny and steeling himself for the trials ahead.

The final blessing of the Mass can be compared to such a moment. Now that may seem counterintuitive, but it's not. Quite the contrary, God's blessing yields great power. During the "movie moment" of the final blessing, God is pointing straight at you. He's looking you in the eye. He is proclaiming to you, and to all the land, that he believes in you and expects great things of you. After all, he just graced and filled you with his very life through the Eucharistic celebration. In this liturgical moment, God gives you more than marching orders; God arms you with his word, his grace, his sword and shield, and his very life—to do battle in the world (Ephesians 6:13-17).

Recessional

The march out of the church may seem "anticlimactic" to many, but it's anything but so. We are being led out by Christ himself to do battle, to wage war, and to declare freedom to those fettered and trapped in sin. Many may miss the symbolic signif-icance of the priest leading us forth, but trained eyes and souls don't. Propelled by the Spirit, we are being called and led forth into God's creation to reclaim what is rightfully his.

All that transpires within the closing moments of the Mass is so amazing that it requires and deserves its own chapter, which you'll read more about next. Put on your dancing shoes. It's time to go to a wedding.

Questions for Reflection and Discussion

1. How often do you bring some intention to Mass, which you can lift up in your heart with the priest as he prays the Eucharistic prayer? How might this practice enrich your experience of Mass?

2. What did you learn or now view differently after reading about the movements and prayers within the Liturgy of the Eucharist? Did anything surprise you? Which moment or moments are most meaningful to you personally?

3. In your own words, describe what receiving Christ in the Eucharist means to you. How has this experience changed for you over the years?

4. How would you explain to someone the importance of stay-ing for the entire Mass and lovingly discourage them from leaving early?

CHAPTER NINE

The Lord of the (Wedding) Rings: Understanding God's Desire for Intimacy

*The greatest love story of all time is
contained in a tiny white host.*
—*Archbishop Fulton Sheen*

There we stood, seven thousand miles from home, in a four-hundred-year-old basilica, offering our lives to one another before an altar of God. We were becoming the sacrament.

Yes, you read that correctly. My wife and I *became* the sacrament. In the Catholic tradition, marriage is far more than two souls pragmatically deciding that it "makes sense" to merge lives and checking accounts. Marriage is far more than an exchange of goods and services. Holy Matrimony is supposed to be just that—holy. Matrimony is a sacrament that a couple doesn't just enter *into* but *becomes*.

While the wedding Mass was perfect, all that led up to it was far from it. Have you ever applied for a marriage license on another continent in a foreign language? How about trying to order flowers from a florist who was long on joy but short on English? Ever try to figure out where to have a small wedding reception dinner in a city you've never visited at an hour they don't serve food? By the time my bride-to-be, our siblings, and

I boarded that plane to hop over the pond to Rome, I wasn't sure if I had successfully arranged for our wedding or inadvertently registered to vote in the next Italian primary.

All of these looming details and unanswered questions went from stresses to graces, however, because when the day arrived and my gorgeous bride walked down the aisle, nothing else mattered to this groom. Truthfully, nothing else mattered to either of us. We had each other, a priest, a church, and some bread and wine. It was God and us, and in God's design, that's the starting point for all marriages.

God's Love Revealed . . . through Marriage

As the great Bishop Fulton Sheen once noted, "It takes three to be married." He said it because he understood something that is often forgotten today: to become all it is intended to be by God, marriage takes three: the man, the woman, *and God*.

> Scripture confirms that marriage is also how God chooses to reveal his great and unconditional love to the world.

There's a reason that God gives us marriage. It isn't "just" for having children, although they are a beautiful fruit of it, to be sure (Psalm 127:3). It isn't "just" to bless us out of our selfishness, although marriage assuredly invites us to grow in virtue. No, Scripture confirms that marriage is also how God chooses to reveal his great and unconditional love to the world.

It's with this reality and, indeed, this understanding of what marriage truly is and what it requires that we take a look at what the Bible teaches us: that the Mass is not just a sacrifice and a family meal; the Mass is a wedding feast.

Have you ever noticed how the Creator uses everything in creation to point us back to him? The divine designer is seen in the sun rising brightly on Martha's Vineyard or setting on the rolling hills of the Emerald Isle. We see God in the powerful glide of a bald eagle in flight or the rapid pace of a hummingbird's wings. God also reveals himself to us through the images used in Scripture: Creator, Author, Master, Potter. No revelatory term, however, is as poignant or all-encapsulating as the image of a Lover and his beloved.

Throughout the Bible, there is no other analogy, no other example, no other image that God employs more to express his love for us than the love between a husband and wife. Quite literally, from Genesis to Revelation, Sacred Scripture is bookended by weddings. Pope Francis has reminded us all that our lives are wrapped up in a "love story"[6]—God's love story—and as Pope St. John Paul II told us on so many occasions, if a marriage is to work, it requires complete surrender and a total gift of self. And the sign of the first covenant between God and Adam and Eve was the Sabbath, which (not coincidentally) also functioned as their wedding day.

Consider, for a moment, these verses and moments within just the Gospels:

- What is the site of Jesus' first public miracle in John 2? A wedding.
- What analogy does Jesus use to teach about fasting in Mark 2? A wedding.

- What backdrop does Jesus use in Luke 12 to teach about humility? A wedding.
- Where is the master returning from in Jesus' parable in Luke 12? A wedding.
- What is the kingdom of heaven likened to by Jesus in Matthew 22? A wedding.
- What are the virgins with the oil lamps preparing for in Matthew 25? A wedding.

The wedding is clearly and repeatedly the analogy of choice, it seems, for our Lord to communicate deep truths regarding his love, his hope for our salvation, and our ultimate end in him.

St. Paul follows the same pattern. In his letter to the church of Ephesus, he draws a clear parallel between marriage and the relationship between Christ and his Church on earth.

Be subject to one another out of reverence for Christ. Wives, be subject to your husbands, as to the Lord. For the husband is the head of the wife as Christ is the head of the church, his body, and is himself its Savior. As the church is subject to Christ, so let wives also be subject in everything to their husbands. Husbands, love your wives, as Christ loved the church and gave himself up for her, that he might sanctify her, having cleansed her by the washing of water with the word, that he might present the church to himself in splendor, without spot or wrinkle or any such thing, that she might be holy and without blemish. Even so husbands should love their wives as their own bodies. He who loves his wife loves himself. For no man ever hates his own flesh, but nourishes and cherishes it, as

Christ does the church, because we are members of his body. (Ephesians 5:21-30)

To be "subject to one another" (Ephesians 5:21) calls not for a domineering love but for a unified love, where the husband and wife become one in more ways than just physically. This subjection is voluntary, mutual, and reciprocal. The selfless love of the husband for his wife is supposed to reveal and model the selfless love of Christ (the bridegroom) for the Church (the bride) (5:25-27). Quite literally, the "mission" of the man is to die for his bride as Christ did for the Church. So marriage in its most biblical and theologically correct sense is not about what a spouse "gets" from the other but, rather what they can give to the other. A marriage is "successful" when there is a deep level of sacrifice, trust, and intimacy between the couple.

The groom's mission is to die for his bride as Christ died for the Church. And what is the woman's role? In a complete contradiction to ancient thinking, which often regarded the wife as far lower or even the property of the man, St. Paul presented a new image. It is one that recognizes and honors the dignity of the woman, just as Christ did (John 4:7-42) and just as St. Paul echoes in other writings (Galatians 3:28). The woman's role is to be "under" the mission ("sub-mission") of the man. The bride must allow the man to lay down his life for her. As she entrusts herself to her husband, she is, by extension, entrusting herself to Christ and honoring the Lord.

The apostle's wordplay likening the man's flesh to his wife (Ephesians 5:29) points us back to the creation story of Genesis (2:24), ensuring that we see the connection to God's original plan of sacrificial love and of the two becoming one flesh (Ephesians 5:31). Remember back in the Garden of Eden before the fall? Remember how everything was "good" with Adam only after the arrival of his equal, Eve? Upon her arrival, things went from good to "very good" (Genesis 1:31), in fact. The "two become one," not figuratively or even just physically, but through mutual self-sacrifice. The couple so vehemently seeks the good of the other that each disappears into the other as they seek God. In this way, properly understood, the arithmetic of the Sacrament of Marriage is $1 + 1 + 1 = 1$, because the man + the woman + God resembles the love of the Trinity, three distinct Persons but one Love.

> Mass is more than a sacrificial meal of thanksgiving. It's a wedding feast.

Obviously, this image of marriage has been misunderstood, hijacked, and watered down in modern culture. It's no wonder, then, that the Mass is so misunderstood even by modern Catholics, because if Christ is the groom and the Church is his bride, Mass is more than a sacrificial meal of thanksgiving. It's a wedding feast.

Renewing Our Vows to God

Christ, the groom, has proposed to the Church, his bride. The ring, the promise of his eternal and undying love, is the new covenant. Through the sacraments, we (the Church) achieve the greatest possible physical intimacy with Christ. We are called into this intimate relationship, that of a pure lover, so that we can become one with God in a forever covenant (remember the Sabbath marriage in chapter 2). Consider these words from the Book of Revelation:

> Then I heard what seemed to be the voice of a great multitude, like the sound of many waters and like the sound of mighty thunderpeals, crying, / *"Hallelujah! For the Lord our God the Almighty reigns. / Let us rejoice* and exult and *give him the glory,* / for the marriage of the Lamb has come, / and his Bride has *made herself ready*; / it was granted her to be *clothed with fine linen, bright and pure"*— / for the fine linen is the righteous deeds of *the saints.*
>
> And the angel said to me, "Write this: *Blessed are those who are invited* to the *marriage supper* of the Lamb." And he said to me, "These are true words of God." Then I fell down at his feet to *worship him.*" (Revelation 19:6-10, emphasis addded)

In this vision that God imparts to St. John (the Book of Revelation is a recounting of St. John's visions), we are given an invaluable insight into the Catholic Mass. Christ, the groom, is coming for his bride, the Church. Note the italicized words. This is liturgical imagery more than wedding imagery; this is a Mass, not just a wedding ceremony.

Not everyone is married or called to marriage. But wedding imagery, more than any other, conveys to us the passion of God for us. God wants intimacy with us. He wants us to let go of any other loves in our life because he knows that no other love can begin to compare to his. God will never let us down. But he wants us to give ourselves to him without reserve. He wants us to live no longer for ourselves, but for him and in him (2 Corinthians 5:15).

In Holy Communion we are called to bring ourselves, with all our imperfections, before the God of the universe and proclaim our need for him. We are to receive his love, as a bride receives the love of her husband. When we walk down the aisle at Mass and hear the words "The Body of Christ," we say, "Amen," meaning, "Yes, I believe." In so doing, we are renewing our vows to God—our baptismal vows—and pledging to forsake all other "lovers" in our lives—anything that separates us from him. We have become one with Christ.

And now we can bear fruit, bringing God's life and proclaiming hope to a world tainted with sickness, depression, and death.

Why would the God of the universe "veil" his mystery and glory in such an unimpressive and common way, in bread and wine? Why would God make himself so humble, so vulnerable, so accessible, so "common"? I'm sure the shepherds outside of Bethlehem and the magi visitors may have wondered the same thing.

Assuredly, it makes no sense to our human thought process. But God foresaw that it wasn't going to make sense, and he reminded us that his thoughts are not our thoughts (Isaiah 55:9-10). It makes no sense unless you seek to understand the heart and mind of God and go all the way back to Eden. He walked with Adam and Even in intimacy (Genesis 3:8), just as he desires to walk with us in the same way. And in the new covenant, in the Eucharist at Mass, the groom, Christ, offers himself unconditionally to us, his bride. He is in us and we are in him. Nothing can separate us except an act of our own will.

So in a sense, the veil that covers the Eucharist is lifted. We can experience the love of Christ in the most intimate way possible.

If we are not experiencing intimacy with Christ in the Eucharist, then we must ask ourselves if we are in a place to receive his love. Maybe we are too consumed with the desire to control how God loves us. Maybe we feel unworthy. Maybe we are not taking the time outside of Mass to really get to know Jesus in Scripture, to sit with him and allow him to gaze upon us in love. We all struggle with accepting God's love, but if we expand our vision—if we see Christ as the lover of our souls and recognize the lengths to which he goes to embrace us—our experience of the Eucharist can grow. Perhaps, like the saints before us, we can understand in some small way just how much Jesus thirsts for us.

Walking Tabernacles

Words matter. It's for this reason that etymology is so important. Learning and understanding what words really mean and what they were originally meant to convey not only deepen our comprehension of the holy Mass but also our experience of it.

Many have heard that the word "Eucharist" is Greek for "thanksgiving," as it should be, for Christ blessed and thanked God for the bread. Additionally, in the context of a meal, it makes perfect sense that we would continually offer thanks to God for what he is providing—his very flesh and blood, his very divine nature (2 Peter 1:4)—at every single Mass.

Now let's look at the Greek word St. Paul continually uses for "grace"—*charis*. Grace, simply put, is God's life *in* us. Now ponder the word "Eucharist" with fresh eyes: Eu*charis*t. Quite literally and sacramentally, this is how Christ puts his very life (grace) within us. Consider this beautiful reality in light of this prophecy from Jeremiah:

> "Behold, the days are coming, says the LORD, when I will make a new covenant with the house of Israel and the house of Judah, not like the covenant which I made with their fathers when I took them by the hand to bring them out of the land of Egypt, my covenant which they broke, *though I was their husband*, says the LORD. But this is the covenant which I will make with the house of Israel after those days, says the LORD: *I will put my law within them*, and I will write it upon their hearts; and I will be their God, and they shall be my people. And no longer shall each man teach his neighbor and each his brother, saying, 'Know the LORD,' for *they shall all know me*, from the least of them to the greatest, says the LORD; for I will forgive their iniquity, and I will remember their sin no more." (Jeremiah 31:31-34, emphasis added)

After we receive the Eucharist, we're encouraged to just sit and be still. We who are filled with God's grace must contemplate the mystery now existing within us, letting the life of God within us grow and mature. As walking tabernacles, we will now be sent forth into a culture desperately in need of the life within us.

My own wedding day was not an end to preparation and expectation. It was, instead, an invitation to a whole new life—one filled with self-sacrifice, surrender, discomfort, and great opportunities to grow in virtue. Marriage is all about the reception of God's grace. The Mass, as a marriage, is all about the reception of God's grace. Notice that we don't "take" Communion as much as we "receive" it.

The sooner we comprehend Communion as a reception with expectation, the sooner we will understand our role in God's plan for salvation and our mission as we leave his house every Sunday to bear fruit in our world.

Questions for Reflection and Discussion

1. When you look at marriages, do you normally "see" or think about God's presence? Why or why not?

2. Why would God use marriage as the primary analogy of his love? What does this say about marriage? About God?

3. Does knowing the meaning and significance of *charis*, or "grace," change or enrich your perception about God's plan for the Eucharist? How does the reception of God's grace— his very life—in the Eucharist change your life outside of Mass?

4. How would you explain the gift of the Eucharist to a non-Catholic Christian? How would you speak about your own experience of receiving Christ in the Eucharist?

CHAPTER TEN

We're on a Mission from God: Understanding Our Role in the Kingdom

Let us go forward in peace, our eyes upon heaven,
the only one goal of our labors.
—St. Thérèse of Lisieux

It was the perfect morning. The kind of morning when you wake up well rested and realize you can lie in bed even longer. No children jumping on the bed. No alarm clock urging you to join the rush-hour melee. Simply a joyful knowledge that you get to enjoy a cup of coffee and pray before heading off to Mass.

This was more than a Sunday morning on vacation without kids for my wife and me. We woke up in paradise—in Maui. You could smell the ocean, hear the breeze, and see the sunrise creeping up over the islands. It was picture-perfect.

As my wife and I slowly rose to greet the day, the bed shook—but it wasn't a vibrating bed. It quickly dawned on us that our vacation was turning into Paradise Lost. Our four-day trip to "heaven" just happened to fall during the first earthquake to hit the islands in twenty years. How's that for timing?

As I held my wife in my arms and the pictures fell from the walls, I became acutely aware of two things. First, we were on the eighth floor of a twelve-story hotel. There were, literally, tons of concrete and mortar above us, so despite my best efforts, I would not be able to shield my wife if the building were to collapse. Second, I found myself thinking something I would have never envisioned myself thinking during our wedding preparation or vows. I actually said to myself, "I wonder if I should throw my wife out that window." There was a pool eight stories below, and in my panic I actually believed that to be an option.

As the tremors subsided and we began our not-so-subdued walk down the flights of stairs, something profound hit me: I care more about my wife's life than my own.

I'm not saying that I love my wife perfectly. She would be the first one to tell you that I have a long way to go. What I am saying was that in a moment when it really counted, I surprised myself. It really was a sacred moment when I saw how the grace of the marriage sacrament had been working in my life. I felt as if I had turned a corner. No longer did I merely proclaim that my spouse was more important than myself; it was actually my default reaction. It sounds funny, but my desire to throw my wife out a window (so to speak) actually demonstrated my desire for her to live and my willingness to die.

I guess you could say that on a morning when "paradise was lost," an even greater paradise was found. God's life—his *grace*—had been working in my soul in unseen ways, ways he let me see when it mattered most. Ironically, my singular concern for my wife's survival revealed that I had made strides in the mission I'd been entrusted with through the power of the sacrament. I was willing to die for my bride; my desire was that she live. In this way I had responded to Christ's call and was, in effect, fulfilling my "mission" as the man.

You Are Sent Forth

As Catholics, we all have a mission, and we're reminded of it at the end of every Mass. It comes from the priest in his words of dismissal, which are said after the closing prayer. In Latin, these words are *Ite missa est* for "Go, it is sent" or, put more simply, "Go, you are sent forth." In the new translation, there are four alternatives that the priest can use; one is "Go forth, the Mass is ended." The response on the part of the assembly is "Thanks be to God" or, in Latin, *Deo gratias.*

> We all have a mission, and we're reminded of it at the end of every Mass.

This final blessing is far more than a two-minute warning signaling the end of Mass. It's a reminder of our mission in the world the other 167 hours each week. It's the King asking us, his knights and ladies, to bow our heads and be blessed for battle before we are led out by Christ (the crucifix, the procession, the priest) into the world like an army of grace-filled soldiers armed only with love. The crucifix is the flag our army marches behind, one that declares a war on sin and selfishness. We enter the Church as many souls, fractured, tired, broken, and hungry, but we exit as one body in Christ, rejuvenated, healed, and fulfilled.

Even the word for "Mass" is a reminder of our mission, since it comes from the Latin word *missa*, which means "to be shot forth." It's the same root word for "missile." *Missa* carries a responsibility, a mission, with it. It's our mission to be soul-seeking missiles, "weapons of Mass instruction" to a world desperately in need of God's truth.

Incidentally, this is yet one more reason not to leave Mass right after Communion. Those who do so break from the community, miss the final blessing, and deny themselves of the graces associated with both.

The Sacraments: A Life-and-Death Situation

The Sacrament of Holy Matrimony destroyed *my life*. Yes, I mean that. Let me explain: the Sacrament of Holy Matrimony destroyed my life *in a beautiful way*. Each of the sacraments brings grace. Grace is God's life, God's very life. So the sacraments offer God's divine life in our daily earthly lives (CCC 1996–97). In order to be filled with God's life, however, *our* lives must first be "emptied."

The sacraments consume us with Christ's life (grace); that is, they eradicate everything that is of "me"—my pride, selfishness, ego, shortsightedness, stubbornness—and leave only what is of God. God's grace shakes us free from the world, leaving only what is of heaven. Ironically, Scripture compares this process to an "earthquake" of sorts (Hebrews 12:26-29).

Through the sacraments, our old life—our former self— is put to death so that God's life will breathe forth from us. God's breathing of his divine life into us (inspiration) leads to our breathing his life out onto others (respiration). We can't breathe without God, nor should we want to do so. Every breath, indeed, every second of every day now becomes holy and sacramental.

As has already been stated, the sacraments flow forth from the Eucharistic sacrifice, from the Last Supper table and the cross. It's through both events, forever linked, that we are to learn not only how to live but how to *die*. Each sacrament now becomes an exercise in both. The intention of matrimony is to show the world, through the couple, what it means to die to yourself and live for each other. The better we understand the "little deaths" required of us on a daily basis and the total mental shift (in perspective) that death to self necessitates, the sooner we'll actually begin to truly live the life to which Christ calls us. Dying to our life so that only Christ's life remains—that is what St. Paul tells us (2 Corinthians 5:15; Galatians 2:20).

God became man for a reason. Jesus' mission was not just to reconcile us and redeem us but to show us how to love properly—to love to the point of death. Following Jesus doesn't just mean emulating his life but also his death. And at the end of the Mass, we are "co-*mission*ed" to share the gifts we've received there. His mission is now *our* mission. The problem is that most of us in the pew don't view the end of Mass that way.

Mission Possible: Using Our Sixth Sense

Several years ago, four little words captivated film audiences around the world: "I see dead people." They were uttered by a frightened young boy in the blockbuster film *The Sixth Sense*. In it we are introduced to a child who "sees" dead people in various scenes and settings throughout his life and who interacts with them and hears their stories. This chilling tale was hailed as cinematic genius for its intensity and plot twists, and today that phrase is all it takes for a generation of moviegoers to recall the film.

To be honest, I see dead people too, though not in the same way.

I see "dead people" every day, souls who are aimlessly walking through life like spiritual zombies. They are breathing but they're not really living. Souls who do not know (nor desire to know) the joy and the freedom offered through a personal and intimate relationship with Jesus Christ are not truly living, not as abundantly as they are designed to live (John 10:10).

We have such people in our offices and schools, in our parishes and ministries, on our teams and in our social circles, and yes, even in our homes. We may even see death when we look in the mirror—not a soul, alive and free, but a body, burdened and fettered, staring blankly back at us. We all go through spiritual droughts. We all have periodic doubts. We are all susceptible to the realities of temptation and the millstone of sin. It's what we do about it that differentiates us. It's about whether we let ourselves be destroyed or whether we keep fighting that makes the difference.

As the Lord reminded Moses, we need only to be still and allow God to fight the battle for us (Exodus 14:14). As the psalmist reminded us, it's in our stillness that we will remember and "know" that he—and he alone—is God (Psalm 46:10). Both of these reminders to the power of stillness, by the way, come in the midst of a battle. We are in a battle for souls, to be sure, beginning with our own. The Lord, however, has armed us with the one weapon we need to emerge victorious and sanctified: prayer, the most powerful weapon in existence.

Before we can fulfill this mission we've been entrusted with and unleash the power of the Eucharistic Body and Blood running through our veins, we have to be sure we're praying before we're moving.

To Be or Not to Be

You can only properly "do" after you've taken time to "be" in prayer. Only then will your life, your vocation, your family, your job, and your ministry (actually, God's ministry *through* you) be rightly ordered. Remember the story of Martha and Mary? It's the classic story of "being versus doing."

> Now as they went on their way, he entered a village; and a woman named Martha received him into her house. And she had a sister called Mary, who sat at the Lord's feet and listened to his teaching. But Martha was distracted with much serving; and she went to him and said, "Lord, do you not care that my sister has left me to serve alone? Tell her then to help me." But the Lord answered her, "Martha, Martha, you are anxious and troubled about many things; one thing is needful. Mary has chosen the good portion, which shall not be taken away from her." (Luke 10:38-42)

Now Martha often gets a pretty bad rap. What was she doing wrong? She was serving the Lord; her hospitality was how she showed her love for God. Truth be told, hospitality was actually the foundation of the entire Mediterranean culture in Jesus' time; it was the highest expectation and form of love in the minds of many. Maybe like Martha, your "love language" is acts of service. You'll find many people like her in parish ministry settings as well, people who are far more comfortable "doing" than praying, serving than "being." It's the great challenge of the Christian life, especially for leaders. It's easier to love others in the name of Christ than it is to just sit and be loved *by Christ* in our daily prayer time.

This is when control freaks (like myself) come unraveled. It's far easier for me to show my love for my wife by accomplishing a "honey-do" list than to just sit on the couch and be "present" to her for long conversations. It's a constant daily struggle for me, the groom, to just slow down and share space with my wife, the bride.

The exact opposite is true of Christ, the bridegroom. He is constantly present, ever available to his bride, the Church. He is waiting and desiring the most intimate relationship possible with each and every one of us. His presence in the Eucharist is an invitation to prayer and, more to the point, to intimacy.

During his visit to Australia for World Youth Day in 2008, Pope Benedict XVI expounded upon this concept that we must first "be" (receive Christ) before we can "do" (offer Christ):

These gifts of the Spirit—a way to participate in the one love of God—are neither prizes nor rewards. They are freely given (cf. 1 Corinthians 12:11). And they require only one response on the part of the receiver: I accept! *Here we sense something of the deep mystery of being Christian. What constitutes our faith is not primarily what we do but what we receive.* After all, many generous people who are not Christian may well achieve far more than we do. Friends, do you accept being drawn into God's Trinitarian life? Do you accept being drawn into his communion of love? (emphasis added)

Do you understand what our former Holy Father means? This is more than just saying, "You can't give what you don't have." In essence, he is saying, "It's better to receive than to give," or for the Christian, "It's necessary to receive Christ and the gifts of the Spirit if you desire to give to others." Otherwise, our giving will be disordered.

Our Church is a church of social justice, as it ought to be. If we are more concerned with serving others food than being fed ourselves by God at his altar table, however, we've lost the essence of the gospel and run the risk of losing God in the process. Our actions and ministry—our very *mission* during the week—is designed to flow *from* the Sunday altar table, not merely toward it. Anyone can serve the poor. Atheists can be far more benevolent than many Christians. What makes us Christian is *why* we do it, *Who* we do it for, and *Who* empowers us to serve!

> Our "doing" will be truly pure because it will be in response to our "being"—our time spent in prayer.

When we pray, however, and when we consistently seek Jesus in the sacraments, most specifically in the Eucharist through Mass and adoration, all our acts of service now flow *from* our interior prayer life and are thus rightly ordered. In short, our "doing" will be truly pure because it will be in response to our "being"—our time spent in prayer. We'll be doing it for the right reason—for God and not for ourselves.

This is a crucially important distinction for modern Catholics, as many of us are better at doing than being. The contemplative life is growing increasingly challenging in our wired culture. How often do we really schedule "contemplation" or prayer in our daily calendars? How often do we view our homes, offices, schools, and other settings as spiritual battlefields? How often do we go to the Lord asking him to reveal to us those he so desperately wants us to reach out to in his name?

The Lord Be with You—Again

Have you ever noticed how often at Mass the priest says, "The Lord be with you"? Four times, to be exact. So why all the repetition?

Many of us in the pews seem to go into spiritual autopilot when we hear the priest say that prayer, reactively uttering, "And with your spirit," without giving it a second thought. But if we really considered what the priest was saying and where that blessing comes from in Scripture, we would take pause. This is not just a blessing; it's a warning and a reminder that what we are about to experience will be a thrilling and terrifying journey of faith. Many times when we hear in Scripture the promise of God's divine presence being with a person, danger follows. Let's take a look at just a few of the times we hear that the Lord "is with" someone in the Bible:

- When Moses is charged in the Midian desert to leave his flocks behind and return to the mighty slave-driving Pharoah with a directive and a warning, the prophet is assured by God that "I will be with you" (Exodus 3:12).

- As Joshua takes command of the remnant Israelite nation and prepares to lead them over the Jordan River against a fierce and overpowering foe, God promises Joshua that "I will be with you" (Joshua 1:5).

- When the Midianites and Amalekites lay siege to Israel, slowly strangling them out of supplies and life, an angel appears to a valiant farmer named Gideon and calls him to war, after assuring him of what? "The LORD is with you" (Judges 6:12).

- As Goliath, the mighty Philistine, towered over the battlefield, taunting the Israelite army, David, the teenaged shepherd and part-time musician, volunteered to fight the warrior. King Saul looked at young David, about to embark on what seemed to be a suicide mission, and said, "Go, and the LORD be with you" (1 Samuel 17:37).

- And when the appointed time had come, the God of the universe sent an angelic envoy to a tiny town called Nazareth, to a virgin betrothed to a local carpenter. The angel greeted the handmaiden with what phrase? "Hail, full of grace, the Lord is with you" (Luke 1:28).

At each stage of the Mass, we see this blessing mean something similar. First, in the beginning of Mass we are warned that we are embarking on a serious and dangerous journey into the heart of God, the upper room of the Passover and the rock-strewn hill of Calvary. *"The Lord be with you."*

Next, after hearing the other Lectionary readings, we stand for the Gospel acclamation. Before its truths are proclaimed for all to hear—truths that are often countercultural and quite "dangerous" to our popularity and the status quo—we are blessed again. *"The Lord be with you."*

Then, during the Eucharistic prayers, we hear it again. Our Lord will soon be present to us in a unique and mystical way. This mystery ought to shake us to the core of our very being. It is a high and great mercy that God veils his true presence to us under the guise of mere bread and common wine, for if our

> We need all the blessing, all the grace, all the power of God that we can get.

hearts perceived the reality of Christ's glory upon that altar, they would explode in ecstasy. We're encouraged to offer up our very lives as he is offering up his. *"The Lord be with you."*

Finally, at the end of Mass we hear it again. *"The Lord be with you."*

It's at that moment that we bow down for God's blessing. Why? Because we need it. We need all the blessing, all the grace, all the power of God that we can get. We are heading out those parish doors, not for coffee and donuts, but to do battle with evil itself. The world is a war zone, and we are being dropped right into the middle of it. Though the Holy Spirit is often depicted as a dove, it might be more accurate to think of him as an F-16 or a B-52, dropping bombs of grace and dropping us as paratroopers of God's love and mercy behind enemy lines.

God has equipped us for a mission, yes, but if we are going to fulfill this mission of love, we have to be aware of what our mission field is and what our tools are.

Putting the "New" in Evangelization

Catholics are talking a great deal about the "New Evangelization"—responding to the call of Popes John Paul II, Benedict, and now Francis. Parishes have put the phrase on their bulletins and banners. Dioceses have set up special offices for the New Evangelization, and the Vatican even convened a Synod of Bishops to discuss it. It's important. It's vital. But how many pew-sitting Catholics across the globe really understand what the New Evangelization means?

The New Evangelization is all about reaching out to the unchurched, but with the sober recognition that this can only happen when Catholics already within the Church wake up. The New Evangelization begins in the pews. We who go to Mass need to behold this sacred mystery with new eyes. Parishes need to reinvest in their people and must do so, first, by reinvesting in good liturgy, liturgy that is as dynamic as it is reverent, that engages the heart and not just the mind.

When it comes to good liturgy or good ministry, it's never an expense: it's an investment. Proverbs tells us, "Where there is no vision, the people perish" (29:18, KJV). In the twenty-first century, however, with parish closings, the priest shortage, and a dwindling number of couples actually getting married in the Church, a more apt translation might be "where there is no vision, the parish will perish." The parish without an inviting and engaging liturgy will perish the fastest. Catholics will wander until they find a parish where they are "fed" spiritually;

like the Israelites in the desert, sadly, many "roaming" Catholics jump from parish to parish or just leave completely. Why would people leave? Where else can someone find all the treasures that the Catholic Church has to offer? Nowhere.

The problem isn't a lack of truth; it's a lack of translation. If we want greater reverence in the pews, we must unearth in the people of God a deeper relevance between what transpires in the sanctuary and the rest of their week. Does the liturgy offer the faithful in the pews a life-altering, soul-shaking, heart-changing encounter with Christ? If not, then why not? Beyond the ongoing catechesis of every person who darkens the doors of the Church, what can we do better today that will transform the Church of tomorrow?

The only thing we really have to offer anyone is Christ in us; everything else will fall short or will fade, rust, break, or die. How truly sad if someone comes to you looking for Christ and finds only you. You have a responsibility that comes with your baptism. You are called to be a saint, or die trying. The French author Leon Bloy once said, "The only real tragedy is not to become a saint." God desperately desires our sainthood and our collective presence in the communion of saints. If God really is the vine and we the branches, we had better start bearing some fruit (John 15:1-8).

So what can you do in a practical way to make this happen? Make and keep Mass a priority. Don't just go for yourself; go for the rest of the family who are gathered there. Don't just show up; arrive with an intention. Sit closer, sing louder, and respond with fervor. Don't just "take" Communion; *receive* Communion. Kneel, but do so with intentionality. Ponder your genuflection.

Let your bows be an outward sign of your interior posture of heart. When you respond, think about the words. When you offer a sign of peace, make sure the recipient knows of your penitence.

Bring others into the Sabbath, *your* sabbath. Realize that the Church exists well beyond your diocesan boundaries, parish parking lot, or personal comfort zone. Reach out and engage your agnostic neighbors. Pray for and dialogue with your atheist co-workers. If your goal is to "keep the peace" and not get overly "religious" with the Thanksgiving conversation, bring it up with extended family one of the other 364 days of the year.

Do it. Allow the Mass to comfort you in your affliction and afflict you where you've grown far too comfortable. Allow God to shake you free of all created (earthly) things and leave only what is heavenly. Only then will you be refined and readied for this mission of love. Only then will you be sure that you're serving in right order, fueled by the Eucharistic table and not by ego or pride. Allow Christ to transform you from the inside out by virtue of his grace-filled Eucharist. Let the Holy Spirit guide you to new depths and greater joy as you allow him to unleash the hidden excellence of your heart.

A sacrifice is an act for another. A gift is not a gift until it is received. Love is not fulfilled until it is shared. And a Catholic remains a Catholic by doing what he was designed to do. You were designed to become "partakers of the divine nature" (2 Peter 1:4). You were designed "for good works" (Ephesians 2:10). You were designed to "die with him," that you may "also live . . . [and] reign with him" (2 Timothy 2:11, 12). You have been "bought with a price" so that you might "glorify God in your body" (1 Corinthians 6:20). You were saved and redeemed by the blood of the Lamb, not so that you would merely breathe, but truly *live*. Put simply, the Eucharist changes *everything* . . . starting with you.

Love is always on a mission—and it is within and through the Catholic Mass that we come to know and fulfill the mission to which God has called us. In this apostolic Church, the Lord calls us to be "fishers of men" (cf. Luke 5:10). That means we must go fishing, not hide in the aquarium.

May God grant us life until our mission is done. Now "go forth" into the world to love and serve the Lord. Amen?

Questions for Reflection and Discussion

1. When you leave church, do you feel as though you have been prepared for a mission? Why or why not?

2. Why is it important to "be" with the Lord before we plunge into active ministry? When have you failed to do so? What was the result?

3. What will you think of this Sunday when you hear these words: "The Lord be with you"? How do you experience God's presence in times of danger or trial?

4. In what ways can you become an evangelist—a fearless and bold "fisher of men"—in your day-to-day life? What opportunities might you have to preach the good news? What opportunities might you be currently missing?

Frequently Asked Questions about the Catholic Mass

1. Why do we "have to go" to Mass?

God didn't "have to" create you, but he did. God could have created each of us to live not on one planet, Earth, but on seven billion separate planets, each of us alone in our own world. But he didn't do it that way. God doesn't "have to" love us as a father; he chooses to do so. God didn't "have to" give us his only Son or his Body and Blood to consume. But his creativity is outshone only by his generosity. Put simply, God doesn't have to love or care for us, but he chooses to do so because he thinks we're worth it.

Is God worth it? Is "rearranging" our Sunday to make time for the God who has blessed us with everything and everyone in our lives worth it? Is having an hour set aside to let God love us while we try to love him worth our time? Are other created things more important to our life (and eternity) than the One who created them?

I like to think about it this way: everything I have is a gift from God, every blessing in my life—every person, every relationship, and every talent. The Mass is also pure gift. The more aware we are of our own sin and our need for a savior, the more clearly we see that the Mass is not merely an obligation but an opportunity—a gift—not to be missed.

2. Is it really a mortal sin to miss Mass?

Why is it a sin to miss Mass? Is the Church blindly audacious or painfully oblivious to suggest that missing Sunday Mass is on the same spectrum of sin as, say, murder or adultery? Perhaps the Church understands things even better than we give her credit for.

Sin is death, we are told by St. Paul (Romans 6:23). Note that the great saint is not speaking metaphorically. No, Scripture clearly teaches that sin is death and grace is life (God's life, as we've already discussed). What great saints had in common was that they preferred physical death and even martyrdom to sin. They understood something that we often forget today, namely, that spiritual death (sin) is far more "deadly" than physical death. Our Lord reminded us not to fear physical death but to avoid spiritual death (sin) at all costs (Matthew 10:28).

The Mass is our source of eternal life. The Mass is the fountain of grace for our dehydrated and self-absorbed souls. Like a grape that withers and dies when cut off from its lifeblood, the vine, so we slowly wither—dying a slow death from sin—when we are not in regular communion with the grace and life of God's vine. So emphatic was Christ about our need for the Father that he used this analogy of the vine and the branches (John 15:1-6).

A "mortal" sin is a sin that is grave in matter. It is one that we know to be a sin and one to which we consent. Missing Mass is absolutely a grave sin, as it cuts us off from God's life-giving and soul-saving grace flowing from the sanctuary (as we've already seen) as well as from our community. The *Catechism* is clear that to miss Mass intentionally and without reason is a grave sin, but it also reminds us that personal sickness or the necessary and charitable caring for another (perhaps an infant or the elderly) may excuse our absence (2181). Under canon law (1245), the priest, too, can offer dispensation from our Sunday Mass obligation for a serious reason.

Missing Mass doesn't just "happen." Choosing to head to a football game or meet friends for breakfast is great, but if in doing so, we miss Mass, we're proclaiming that we are actually the god around which our Sunday revolves. For where our treasure is, there will our hearts be also (Matthew 6:21). Fortunately, most parishes offer multiple Mass times (including the Saturday vigil or even Sunday evening Mass) to accommodate our overly busy schedules. So yes, missing Mass is a mortal sin. The question we should be asking, however, is not, "Is it deadly to miss?" but rather, "How could I ever miss Mass when God is giving himself to me in such a profound way?"

3. How late can I arrive for Mass and still have it "count"?

How many cigarettes can one smoke before getting cancer? How much fried food can one consume before having to schedule an angioplasty? How often can I call in sick before I get fired? The virtue of prudence is rooted not only in finding the right answer but, more to the point, in asking the right question.

Asking how late we can arrive for Mass is like asking, "How far is too far?" when it comes to sexuality. We want to know where to draw the line so that we can more easily and readily tap dance around it. Technically, if you arrive after the Gospel has begun, it wouldn't "count" as fulfilling your Sunday obligation. The stipulation is not intended to be a pass or a reward for laziness, selfishness, or tardiness. While sometimes walking in late is beyond our control, it can usually be avoided by a more responsible and intentional approach to how we prepare for Mass and when we go. The Mass begins long before the car pulls into the space or the behind hits the pew. Our Mass experience begins in the days leading up to Sunday, when we are reading the upcoming Scripture passages and preparing our hearts to receive the God of the universe.

4. Is it a sin to miss Mass when I'm on vacation?

The short answer: yes, it's a sin to miss Mass, even if you're on vacation.

Here's the long answer.

Imagine your father calling you and inviting you on a week-long, all-expenses-paid vacation. First-class plane tickets, five-star hotel, all-you-can-eat buffets—everything is paid for, a blessing beyond comprehension. His only stipulation is that you join him for dinner one night.

You decide to accept the blessing of the vacation, but you stand up your father for dinner. Your excuse: you couldn't find the restaurant because you were from out of town. Your father knows that you have GPS on your phone and that the hotel has a concierge, a local directory in every room, and free Wi-Fi.

What have you communicated to your father, not only about the blessings, but also about your relationship?

5. How long am I supposed to fast before Mass and why?

Have you ever peered at a clock on Sunday morning and done the math in your head before running out the door to Mass? Technically, we are called to fast from food for at least an hour before receiving Communion. Some try to fast for an hour before the Mass begins, and I know priests who encourage fasting the entire morning until after Mass has concluded.

But why? We unite our quite minimal sacrifice of fasting to the sacrifice of Christ within the Mass. When we fast, we help our bodies and souls to function in right order, with the spirit leading the flesh and not vice versa. The desert fathers taught fasting as part of their formation of monks. The belief was that if a man could not first temper his own desire for food, he might never be able to temper his appetite for sex when called to a life of celibacy.

Fasting before Mass helps ensure that we come hungry, literally and figuratively, and that Christ—and nothing (and no one) else—satisfy that hunger.

6. Why does a priest (or deacon) preach after the Gospel reading?

Our priests, while not all Scripture scholars or moral theologians, have the daunting task of taking the timeless truth of Scripture (penned between two thousand and five thousand years ago) and helping to "translate" it into present-day terms every Sunday. For example, how does one fulfill Christ's command to reach out to lepers when there don't seem to be any lepers hanging out in front of your local coffee shop? In the homily, the priest or deacon is trying to ensure that we not only comprehend the often confusing context of the readings but that we understand the Church's wisdom on matters of faith and morals and are aware of the implications and the need to live them out faithfully *and immediately*.

St. Paul discussed the importance of receiving and living out the word:

> And we also hank God constantly for this, that when you received the word of God which you heard from us, you accepted it not as the word of men but as what it really is, the word of God, which is at work in you believers. (1 Thessalonians 2:13)

The homily ought to help us live out God's word more intentionally in deed and not merely in thought.

7. Why do we sometimes use incense at Mass?

Like many traditions within the Mass, the reason we did something centuries ago is not necessarily the reason we continue to do it. Incense not only served a liturgical function but a practical purpose in the early Church, masking the odor within the worship space. As the early Church experienced persecution, believers were forced to meet in less-than-ideal surroundings (like catacombs). Incense was a practical necessity when the stench of death or disease filled the air or when many bodies were crowded tightly in hot and humid spaces.

As the Bible reminds us, however, the use of incense was not just a strictly practical matter. Since Old Testament times, the use of incense has been consistent with worship. Offering or burning incense to God was a custom used not only by the Jewish people but by almost every empire and world power in antiquity. In the Book of Maccabees, for instance, we see the Greek soldiers trying to force the Jews to burn incense to their false gods. Incense was associated both with the worship of the divine and with the priestly office. Recall that the magi brought Christ gold, myrrh, and frank*incense*.

So when we burn incense at Mass, it is, in part, an outward sacramental sign of worship. We are reminded (as the psalms tell us) that as the smoke rises to the heavens, so do our prayers (see Psalm 141:2, for instance). The smoke within the sanctuary almost creates a "veil" between the heavenly and earthly realities that are, in fact, meeting, drawing our senses toward and into the sacred mystery we are beholding before us.

8. What if I don't like to sing?

If you don't like to sing, I'd recommend avoiding karaoke bars, but that personal preference has nothing to do with the Mass. The Mass isn't a concert for those who like to sing, any more than it is a curse for those who despise it. The Mass is about far more than the music, but the music helps us to pray (or it should) more deeply and more freely.

Oftentimes we are inhibited from singing publicly because we are self-conscious about the sound of our voices. Don't let a seeming lack of musical ability or vocal range deter you! If God has blessed you with a phenomenal voice, one that makes the heavenly host stand up and take notice, then good—praise God with it! If, however, you were absent the day that heaven was handing out vocal range, fret not (pun intended). If God did not bless you with an amazing singing voice, there is no better time or way to get back at God with it than during the Mass.

In all seriousness, you can pray the Mass without singing, but what a glorious statement, example, and prayer it is when you do sing. So cast off your fears, sacrifice your personal discomfort on the altar of public opinion, and offer it up to the Lord. St. Paul's words to the church in Ephesus are as important today as they were two thousand years ago:

> Be filled with the Spirit, adressing one another in psalms and hymns and spiritual songs, singing and making melody to the Lord with all your heart, always and for everything giving thanks in the name of our Lord Jesus Christ to God the Father. (Ephesians 5:18-20)

9. Why doesn't the Catholic Church just "get with the times" and update the Mass?

There's an old joke that goes like this: "How many Catholics does it take to change a light bulb?" The answer: "Change?"

The joke is obviously meant to demonstrate that the Catholic Church does not change nearly as quickly, readily, or frequently as most other entities in the world, which is true because the Church is not of this world; its headquarters is in heaven.

Perhaps a more appropriate rendition of the joke would be this: "How many Catholics does it take to change a light bulb?" The answer: "None. We use candles."

But back to the question: why doesn't the Church change the Mass? Because the Mass is timeless, and as you've seen in this book, the Mass is far more than just the sum of its parts.

We don't use candles today for light as those in the early Church once did. We keep them, however, because of what they symbolize and remind us of. In a way, candles make present a past reality. Throughout the Mass, the movements, prayers, rituals, and exchanges usher the past into the present while pointing us all toward our collective future—heaven.

Put simply, newer ideas are not always the best ideas. In truth, older ideas are often superior because they have stood the test of time. Thinking that something is always better because it is newer can be a narrow-minded and prideful way of looking at things. Appreciating where we have come from and those who have brought us to where we are is usually a more respectful and humble stance. Some traditions within the Mass can and do change with and over time, because liturgy is organic and dynamic. Some are so timeless that to alter them would undoubtedly diminish our perception of all else that is transpiring upon that altar.

10. Why can't I stay at home and pray by myself?

You can. In fact, you're encouraged to pray without ceasing (1 Thessalonians 5:17), to pray at home and when you're out and about (Deuteronomy 6:6-7).

There are 168 hours in the week, however, and spending one or two with the rest of the family at the house and table of the Lord is not meant to hamper or hinder your prayer life but to bless and broaden it.

Christ calls us to be one body, one family of God. Our actions affect others:

> The cup of blessing which we bless, is it not a participation in the blood of Christ? The bread which we break, is it not a participation in the body of Christ? Because there is one bread, we who are many are one body, for we all partake of the one bread. (1 Corinthians 10:16-17)

In short, as a Catholic Christian, personal prayer and communal prayer are not "either/or" propositions; they are "both/and" invitations. You are called to have a robust and daily personal prayer life, yes. You are not, however, an only child; you are part of a larger family we call the Church, and as such, your presence is desired around the family dinner table. In this family, we don't eat dinner in our bedrooms or in front of the television. We sit up straight, participate, and eat what the Father provides. (Can you tell that I'm a father?)

11. Why do I have to give money to the Church?

As was mentioned in chapters 4 and 8, we give alms at Mass as part of our sacrifice to God. In the early Church, the collection at Mass was taken up for the needs of the poor. Today the collection also supports the operations of the parish.

The Church does not specify how much you are to give. However, some Catholics have decided to tithe a percentage of their income for both the Church and other charities. "Tithe" is an Old English term that derives from the Hebrew word *aser*, meaning "ten," or *ma'aser*, meaning "the tenth part." The "one-tenth" comes from an early scene with Abram (later known as Abraham):

> And Melchizedek king of Salem brought out bread and wine; he was priest of God Most High. And he blessed him and said, "Blessed be Abram by God Most High, / maker of heaven and earth; / and blessed be God Most High, / who has delivered your enemies into your hand!" And Abram gave him a tenth of everything. (Genesis 14:18-20)

Notice that Abram gives a tenth of *everything* (in modern financial terms, that's 10 percent of gross, not net, income). This functions as a model for us all. It is a way of showing God and reminding ourselves that we must never put creation above the Creator nor forget where all our gifts ultimately come from (James 1:17).

Collecting money supports the work of the Church:

> Now concerning the contribution for the saints: as I directed the churches of Galatia, so you also are to do. On the first day of every week, each of you is to put something aside and store it up, as he may prosper, so that contributions need not be made when I come. (1 Corinthians 16:1-2)

When we tithe a certain percentage of our income to our local parish, the needs of the parish (and extended local) community are served, and our pastor can count on us—he knows how much we will be contributing each month. As part of our tithe, we should also consider giving to a charity or ministry that builds up God's kingdom on earth. How much to tithe should be prayerfully considered each year, based on what God is calling you to do and what circumstances you are facing that year.

12. Why won't the Church ordain women?

This is a popular question among Catholics today (and even non-Catholics). The perception is that for cultural reasons or because of discrimination, women have been prevented from serving as priests over the centuries by a male-dominated hierarchy within the Vatican. The truth, however, is that the pope couldn't ordain women even if he wanted to, because it is Christ, not the Church, who set apart the priesthood for men. Pope St. John Paul II made it clear in *Ordinatio Sacerdotalis* that "the Church has no authority whatsoever to confer priestly ordination on women" (4), reiterating that Christ chose only men to fulfill the priestly office and function. God took flesh as a man. Christ, being a man, shares his priesthood with men. When the priest stands and offers the sacrifice at Mass, he is doing so *in persona Christi,* which means "in the person of Christ." The male priest is offering Christ his own body to work through.

Some have argued that Jesus was somehow "unable" to ordain women as his priests due to the cultural norms of the

Mediterranean culture and Semitic world, but those assertions are frightfully shortsighted. Jesus violated the norms of his day almost daily. He raised the dignity of women by reaching out to them, healing them, bringing them into his close company, and allowing them to minister to him. Throughout Christ's earthly ministry, we see him treating women with every bit of the respect they deserved, even when those around him failed to do so. So why, then, would Jesus reserve his priesthood for men?

The answer lies in God's divine plan for salvation and for his Church. While men and women are absolutely equal, we are, still, quite different in genetic and physiological makeup and vocational purpose. As a man, I could just as easily and readily ask the Lord why he allows only women to carry and bear children. The argument could be made that men are strong enough and just as "able" to carry a child, so why didn't God allow *that* in his divine plan? This side of heaven, we won't ever know.

What we do know, however, is that from the beginning, God gave men and women different roles but one goal: sainthood. The highest calling of life is not to become a priest but to become a saint. Let's not forget that the greatest saint, the Queen of heaven, was a woman—and a stay-at-home mom at that.

13. Why do I need to be absolved of any mortal sin before going to Communion?

Imagine yourself on Christmas morning opening presents. You are given a gift from your father that cost him his life savings. He places it into your hands with great care. You are overwhelmed by the beauty not only of the gift but of the great sacrifice and love that are behind it. You are speechless at how this gift could be entrusted to you. At this moment, you rise, exit the room, drag the gift through the mud outside, and throw it in a dirty trunk filled with junk and trash.

Of course you don't, because doing so would make absolutely no sense.

Our actions follow our beliefs. If we believe something is a true gift, we handle it with care and offer it the great respect that it undoubtedly deserves. By extension, sin pushes out God's grace, suffocating God's life within us, darkening our intellect, and sullying our souls. If we have serious (mortal) sin that is not reconciled, we have refused to clean out our spiritual "trunk," and as a result, we are in no condition to receive the perfect, stainless, and unfathomable gift of the Eucharist until our spiritual house is in order. The Sacrament of Confession not only prepares a proper receptacle for God's grace, but it transforms us, once again, into a monstrance—a mobile tabernacle ready and able to bring Christ's Eucharistic presence into the world.

St. Paul provides the church in Corinth an even more succinct answer to this question:

> Whoever, therefore, eats the bread or drinks the cup of the Lord in an unworthy manner will be guilty of profaning the body and blood of the Lord. Let a man examine himself, and so eat of the bread and drink of the cup. For any one who eats and drinks without discerning the body eats and drinks judgment upon himself. (1 Corinthians 11:27-29)

14. How do I to tell my non-Catholic friends and family that they can't receive Communion?

When a non-Catholic friend or family member comes with us to Mass, we hope they have a great experience. We pray for good music, stellar preaching, and friendly faces. But if we haven't fully prepared our guest, a very awkward moment may ensue when the usher gets to our pew, everyone stands to get in line to receive Communion, and our guest follows. We are trapped in a horribly uncomfortable situation that could have been avoided.

The Catholic Church rightly teaches that those at Mass who are not Catholic or who are not in a state of grace should abstain from receiving the Eucharistic Body and Blood and, instead, ask for a blessing or make a spiritual communion. Oftentimes non-Catholic visitors tend to view this as a slight of sorts or as a judgmental lack of hospitality or charity on the part of the Church when, in fact, nothing could be further from the truth.

In saying that non-Catholics may not receive the Eucharist, the Church is actually showing incredible respect and asking others to do likewise. When we go forward to receive the Lord, we precede that reception with an interaction. The priest, deacon, or Eucharistic minister elevates our Lord and, making eye contact with us, proclaims, "The Body of Christ." The faithful respond, "Amen."

That exchange is far more than ecclesial protocol or going through the liturgical motions. It is a proclamation of Christ's true presence, a humble reception of God's forever sacrifice, and, ultimately, an affirmative profession of our entire Creed.

In reserving the reception of the Eucharist to those who have been catechized in the faith and have prayerfully received the sacraments within the fullness of the Catholic faith, we are ensuring the dignity of the sacrament while simultaneously protecting others from abandoning their entire belief system!

This is no mere moment within the Mass during which we want everyone to feel included or to avoid embarrassment. This is the moment when we proclaim, once again, who we are and *whose* we are. In this moment, we unite ourselves with the perfect love of God in the Eucharistic embrace. To allow others to partake without fully understanding, believing, or proclaiming the same is a disservice to them. If they do believe that Christ is fully present in the Eucharist, then it is high time they enroll in the RCIA class at the parish. If they do not believe, then we should not put them in the awkward position of proclaiming, "Amen."

Ultimately, the best thing we can do is to have the conversation long before Mass begins. Invite anyone and everyone to Mass with you, and reassure them that they are always welcome. In doing so, share the beauty and glory of the Lord's true presence in such a way that they see the theological significance and personal relevance on your part. They may just be so taken by the depth of your love for the Eucharist that they will, one day, seek such an intimate union for themselves. That is the kind of witness St. Peter encourages us to make (1 Peter 3:15).

15. What's the problem with leaving right after Communion?

There are many jokes about how "good" Catholics are at making people feel guilty. I've been in parishes, for instance, that have signs posted that read, "Remember, Judas left first too." The idea is that such signs will act as a deterrent for people leaving early from Mass—right after they receive Communion. While those signs might keep someone from leaving early, I'd argue that they're likely to keep them from wanting to come back.

I hear it from both sides. I hear priests verbally admonish early exit-ers about how God is not "fast food." I hear parishioners complain that there are too many special announcements and presentations at the end of Mass. I watch slow-going, elderly people exit early, hoping to avoid overwhelming foot traffic, and jersey-clad football fans looking to avoid parking-lot traffic. At the end of the day, however, we offer our time to that which we view as important.

Communion is not the end of Mass. In fact, the time of meditation and prayer following Communion is one of the most important moments, not only within the liturgy, but within our entire week. The Eucharistic meditation provides us with unrivaled intimacy and spiritual communion. The final blessing carries with it great grace that we will desperately need to live out the gospel challenge we've just heard. The announcements (if there are any) invite us to be part of the parish family the other 167 hours of the week, and the final song, while technically not part of the Mass, is a great way to raise our voices and celebrate God's greatness once again.

In short, if we really understood what was transpiring at Mass, we would not be in such a hurry to leave. We'd be embracing every minute in the pew and every chance to stay in God's throne room, surrounded by the saints—past and future.

If so many are exiting early that the pews appear half-filled following Communion, then the priest and his staff have far more work to do in evangelizing the parish and in encouraging parishioners to more fully comprehend and appreciate the gift of the liturgy. Guilt, however, is never the path to achieve the desired end.

16. How do I get my teen to go? When do I stop forcing my kids to go?

After working in youth ministry for more than twenty years, I can honestly say that this is the most frequent question I receive from parents. Sometimes parents begin to lose heart and want to give up rather than have the weekly fight over Mass attendance. And well-intentioned but obviously frustrated parents start to believe that their growing teenagers should "be allowed to decide for themselves," or that the fight does more harm than good.

While I understand that mode of thinking and I don't relish "the fight" either, it is dangerous on multiple levels.

First, I remind parents that they are just that—parents. We are not called to be our teenagers' friends. When that happens, the parent/child relationship becomes disordered, and respect is forever lost.

Second, if parents were married in the Catholic Church, they made a vow to God to raise their children "according to the teachings of Christ and his Church." Faithful participation in the Mass is part of that expectation. Parents may not be able to control what a child does after he leaves home, but they can certainly make clear what their expectation is while that child is living at home.

Third, that being said, parents have to keep it positive. Children, especially teenagers, will reject a "do as I say, not as I do" philosophy. If we want our teens to engage more fully in the Mass or in their Catholic faith, then we (as the parents) have to do so too. They should see our love for God woven through our conversations, through the rhythm and prayer of our day, and in our demeanor. Our love for the faith and for Christ ought to be seen clearly in every Sign of the Cross, genuflection, and meditation during the Mass. We, as parents, must become what we desire our children to be: saints in the making.

Finally, the more we make Sundays about the family and not just about "getting to church," the easier all of this will become. We must stop "squeezing in" Mass between games, recitals, activities, and events, and instead make it the family-centered lynchpin of our week. Eliminating any and all distractions from family time on Sundays may hurt a little at first, but it will save our families in the long run, and it may just become the foundation of faith that our teens will build their lives on in college and long after.

Ten Ways to Get More
Out of Mass

1. Get the lay of the liturgical land.

In other words, get to know your Catholic family home that is your parish. Stop by between Monday and Saturday when Mass is not going on. Bring your kids or grandkids along for the tour. Slowly and prayerfully engage in every element. Contemplate the crucifix. Survey the stained glass more closely. Stop to appreciate every statue. Draw near to the sanctuary and take it all in. Pause at the baptismal font to thank God for the gift of your own baptism. Kneel in humble appreciation for the Lord's perpetual presence, symbolized by the flickering red candle burning brightly beside the tabernacle. The more intentionally you "see" the church's environment with the eyes of faith and the people oe purpose that each element signifies, the more deeply you'll be able to "enter into" the Mass when Christ does.

2. Be sure to read ahead.

Read all four readings—yes, all *four* readings (don't forget the psalm response) ahead of time. Beginning on Monday, start reading the upcoming Sunday Mass readings. Perhaps you can read all four on Monday and then again throughout the week, or maybe you can take one reading a day and journal about it. Spend time with footnotes or commentaries on each, drawing more deeply into the true meaning behind the words. Take advantage of free audio and video podcasts that are available to help you (my own free podcasts are available at biblegeek.com). Doing this not only ensures you'll know what is happening during the first half of the Mass, but it will also take away any pressure at the moment when the lector is reading. If a baby wails or your mind wanders (as happens sometimes), you needn't worry; you will have already read and studied God's word in eager anticipation of that moment. I also encourage Catholic parents to allow their children to bring their Bibles to Mass. My seven-year-old takes a compact Bible with her to Mass every Sunday and follows along with the lector. Not only is she learning to navigate the books of the Bible, but she is more engaged in the Mass and is retaining the message far more.

3. Pack your bags.

Many say they don't get anything out of Mass, but maybe it's because they fail to first bring anything to it. Mass is a time to bring your issues, stresses, anxieties, fears, concerns, and personal baggage. Check your bags at the foot of the sanctuary! Bring a special intention with you, someone or something you want to offer up to the Lord upon his altar alongside the gifts. The Lord is offering up his very life for you. What are you willing to offer up to him so that you might follow and love him even more perfectly?

4. Get wet.

Don't just reactively reach for the holy water upon entering and exiting. Make the gesture intentional. As you reach, remember the transformative power of the sacraments. Thank God for the gift of your baptism, by which you have the privilege of being called God's son or daughter. As you trace the sign of the cross upon your body, contemplate how water brings both death and life, and consider how important it is to be covered by and filled with God's grace through the sacraments.

5. Sit up.

As in, "sit up closer." The old adage that good Catholics sit in the back might make for a well-timed punch line from Father, but ask yourself why people want front-row seats at concerts and games and the back row at Mass. The closer you can get to the sanctuary, the better view you'll have of heaven visiting earth by the power of the Holy Spirit. While you're at it, don't just sit closer to the front, but change seats frequently from one Sunday to the next. Many Catholics (my parents included) always had "their pew" over the years. The more you switch seats, however, the more you come to know your fellow parishioners as your brothers and sisters in the faith.

6. Strike a chord with God.

While they may open the hymnal, too many Catholics take the word "refrain" far too literally. If God gave you a beautiful voice, praise him with it. If God gave you a horrible voice, sing anyway. Remember that you're not just singing; you're lifting your voice, mind, and heart to your heavenly Father. Music doesn't just incline the ear to God; it directs the soul back to him. St. Augustine said that when we sing, we pray twice. Set the tone for others through your example. The Mass is assuredly more than music, and many parishes can undoubtedly "do music" better, but the best way to improve it is to participate in it. If you can sing or play an instrument and haven't yet volunteered to join the choir or music ministry, do so. Anyone can point out the problem, but only those with musical gifts can become part of the solution.

7. Go through with your heart transplant.

Are you really putting your heart upon that altar with the gifts of bread and the wine? Are you *really* giving God permission to have his way with you, entrusting him with your health, your finances, your job, your marriage, your children, your vocation, and your future? Are you Christ falling on your knees in the Garden of Gethsemane, heralding that the Father's will be done, or are you one of the disciples who fell asleep? At Mass, Christ is offering you redemption, a time to exchange your tired, sin-tattered heart for his exuberant, grace-filled sacred heart. Take him up on his offer upon the altar. Give God permission to transform your heart, not just the gifts.

8. Say it like you mean it.

Extend a hand or a kiss of peace as though it's your last chance to right a wrong. Offer genuine forgiveness to family members and friends who have wronged you, and seek humbly the forgiveness of others. This is a great warm-up for heaven. This is for the dads who yelled in the car on their way to Mass and the moms who ran out of patience an hour before the opening prayer. This is for the kids who talked back that morning and the friend who upset you greatly the night before. The kiss of peace isn't just a time to "get right" with one another but also to give others permission to hold you to a higher standard. It demonstrates your humility as well as God's grace actively at work in you.

9. Relish the silence.

You know when those silent moments are coming. Relish them. Silence, properly understood, is not our gift to the Father but his gift to us. It's in these intimate moments that we, like the beloved disciple at the Last Supper, draw near to our Lord and rest our heads upon his breast. The saints remind us that it is in these moments that we are closest to God within our day or week.

10. Go forth with purpose.

Do you leave Mass with a mission? There are people who desperately need what you have! Before you exit that pew, before your genuflection is complete, and before you deactivate the car alarm in the parish parking lot, have a goal, a purpose, and a plan. Who are you going to invite next week? Who are you going to reach out to at work or school? What do you need to work on personally, and how do you plan to unleash the powder keg of grace within your soul in the coming hours and days? The question is not whether you have been empowered at Mass but whether you comprehend the power that exists within you—and what you plan to do about it.

Endnotes

1. Scott Hahn, *A Father Who Keeps His Promises* (Cincinnati, OH: Servant Books), 1998, 62–63.

2. This quote is translated in various ways. Here is how it is translated on the Vatican website: "The ways of the Lord are not easy, but we were not created for an easy life, but for great things, for goodness." It is from Pope Benedict XVI's April 25, 2005, address to German pilgrims who had come to Rome for his inauguration ceremony. The speech can be accessed at http://www.vatican.va/holy_father/benedict_xvi/speeches/2005/april/documents/hf_ben-xvi_spe_20050425_german-pilgrims_en.html.

3. I recall the first time I heard this story told publicly by Dr. Scott Hahn. It moved my heart but left my mind skeptical. "Could Pope John Paul II be *this* amazing?" I asked myself. A few years later, as my bride and I received his papal blessing, all doubt was removed. Kneeling before John Paul the Great, peering into his eyes and clutching his hand, I can honestly say I've never encountered such a soul. My own was forever changed by my encounter of Christ within him. Dr. Hahn did confirm this story in a recent phone conversation.

4. N.T. Wright, *Following Jesus* (Grand Rapids, MI: William B. Eerdmans Publishing Co.), 1995, 9.

5. Cyprian of Carthage, Treatise 1, *On the Unity of the Church*.

6. Taken from Pope Francis' weekday homily of April 24, 2013, accessed at http://www.news.va/en/news/pope-francis-church-is-in-a-love-story.

T his book was published by The Word Among Us. Since 1981, The Word Among Us has been answering the call of the Second Vatican Council to help Catholic laypeople encounter Christ in the Scriptures.

The name of our company comes from the prologue to the Gospel of John and reflects the vision and purpose of all of our publications: to be an instrument of the Spirit, whose desire is to manifest Jesus' presence in and to the children of God. In this way, we hope to contribute to the Church's ongoing mission of proclaiming the gospel to the world so that all people would know the love and mercy of our Lord and grow ever more deeply in love with him.

Our monthly devotional magazine, *The Word Among Us*, features meditations on the daily and Sunday Mass readings, and currently reaches more than one million Catholics in North America and another half million Catholics in one hundred countries around the world. Our book division, The Word Among Us Press, publishes numerous books, Bible studies, and pamphlets that help Catholics grow in their faith.

To learn more about who we are and what we publish, log on to our website at www.wau.org. There you will find a variety of Catholic resources that will help you grow in your faith.

Embrace His Word, Listen to God . . .

www.wau.org